Luis Alonso-Schoekel

CELEBRATING THE EUCHARIST

Biblical Meditations

CROSSROAD • NEW YORK

1989

The Crossroad Publishing Company
370 Lexington Avenue, New York, N.Y. 10017

Original title: *Meditaciones biblicas sobre la Eucaristia.* Editorial Sal Terrae, Santander 1986.

Translated from the Italian by
John Deehan & Patrick Fitzgerald-Lombard.

Printed in the United States of America

Library of Congress Cataloging-in-Publication Data

Alonso-Schoekel, Luis.
[Meditaciones biblicas sobre la Eucaristia. English]
Celebrating the Eucharist : biblical meditations / Luis Alonso-Schoekel.
p. cm.
Translation of: Meditaciones biblicas sobre la Eucaristia.
ISBN 0-8245-0938-2
1. Mass—Meditations. 2. Bible—Meditations. 3. Lord's Supper (Liturgy)—Mediations. 4. Catholic Church—Liturgy—Meditations.
I. Title.
BX2230.2.A4413 1989
264'.0203—dc19 88-36639
CIP

CONTENTS

PREFACE

In different circumstances, at very different latitudes and longitudes, I have had occasion to expound a few simple biblical reflections on the Eucharist. I have sought, with these, to communicate the experience of one who studies the Bible, especially the Old Testament, and who wants to live the Eucharist.

I was surprised by the interest with which my reflections were received. Was it because of some novelty, on account of their biblical contribution? Was it because of the love of the Eucharist and the desire to penetrate ever more deeply into its mystery?

Now that my publishing activity has reached the age of forty books, I wanted to celebrate this birthday with a tiny offering. As at the Offertory, I want to present it along with the simple gifts of bread and wine. My reflections too are the fruit of the earth and work of human hands. I hope that through this approach they may receive a little grace, to be able to share it with my brothers with whom I share the Eucharist, that on them may descend, in the end, the blessing of the Trinity as the guarantee of fruitfulness.

My offering is tiny both in comparison with the greatness of the theme and also because my reflections are neither rigorous nor systematic. Perhaps the greatest service which they can offer is to refer the reader to systematic and scientific studies.[1]

I thank Sister Eugenia Soler for her collaboration.

Fr L. Alonso-Schoekel

[1] M. Gesteira Garza, *La Eucaristía, misterio de comunión*, Madrid 1983; J.M. Sánchez Caro, *Eucaristía y historia de la salvación*, Madrid 1983.

1. THE SIGN OF THE CROSS

1. 'In the name of the Father and of the Son and of the Holy Spirit'. So begins the Mass and so begin many of our actions. We take no notice of what we are doing, because we are in a hurry to pray. We think that making the sign of the cross is not praying, but simply a gateway leading to prayer. Not that we are waving our arms in the air in an unrecognizable gesture; we do it correctly, but without calm, or without particular attention, because we want to recite a Hail Mary or an Our Father, or because we are beginning to celebrate Mass. Yet few moments of prayer are so intense, so concentrated, as making the sign of the cross.

Let us imagine tourists climbing the steps of the Cathedral of Santiago. Watching them hurry through the portico to enter the nave, one would be tempted to grab them by the arm, stop them and hold them back in the gateway of glory, the glory of those apostles of stone who greet and welcome the visitors. Something like that is the making of the sign of the cross: it is a magnificent portico through which we enter gloriously into prayer.

In Spanish we have two verbs and two gestures: 'santiguarse' (to make the sign of the cross) and 'persignarse' (to sign oneself). 'Santiguar' means to sanctify or consecrate: it takes the form of a sign of the cross and a trinitarian invocation. 'Persignarse' is a cumulative and repetitive action, as in *per*suading, *pur*suing or *per*turbing, and refers more appropriately to the triple cross 'on the forehead, on the lips and on the breast'. The words which are spoken are a request for protection: 'Through the sign of the holy cross, free us from our enemies, Lord'. Here the motive is one of protection, in contrast to the sign of the cross which has the purpose of consecration.

In this first reflection I would like to dwell on the sign of the cross with the trinitarian invocation which comes at the beginning of our celebration of the Eucharist. There are two elements to consider: the *sign* and the *name*.

2. *The sign* is a very ancient cultural usage which retains its effectiveness today. Sign, mark, badge, label, inscription, nameplate etc.; the variety of synonyms indicates the many forms in which this phenomenon is found.

Excavations in the lands of the Ancient East have brought to light jar handles on which letters and signs are impressed. These could indicate the producer or the owner of a product – grain, wine, oil produced and harvested by N., or property of N. Innumerable seals in cylindrical shape come from Mesopotamia, and others in the form of scarabs from Egypt. The artist inscribed on these a design or a picture as a negative: it was a work in miniature, sometimes exquisitely done. The cylinder was rolled on a soft material, and the picture was impressed as a positive image. There were seals too in the form of rings, and others which hung from the neck or the wrist. They could have belonged to a king, a minister or a secretary, and they were used for legal purposes on documents. The delegation of authority could be accompanied by the giving of one's personal seal.

The Old Testament also confirms this usage:

'Pharaoh took off his signet ring and put it on the hand of Joseph' (Gen 41:42), delegating to him his imperial authority. Jezebel 'wrote letters in the name of Ahab, sealed it with his seal, then sent it to the elders and leaders of the city' (1 Kings 21:8). The King Ahasuerus said to Esther and to Mordecai, 'You may write as you think best, in the name of the king, and seal it with the king's ring, because what is written in the name of the king and sealed with the king's seal is irrevocable' (Esther 8:8; cf. 3:12). Earlier the Patriarch Judah carried his personal ring secured with a cord (Gen 38:18.25). Jeremiah uses the image of the seal to indicate a very personal belonging of the king to the Lord: 'As I live, says the Lord, even if Jehoiakim was a signet ring on my right hand, I would tear him off' (Jer 22:24). According to the prophet Haggai, the Lord says to Zerubbabel: 'I will make you like my seal, because I have chosen you' (Haggai 2:23).

So this then is its origin and setting: an edict coming from a king, or a person's household property. The usage remains today in a different form. A great part of advertising, if not all, is based on the trade-mark which the consumer must recognize. We see a circle with three spokes, and we recognize the make of the car; the same happens for detergents, drinks and films. There is the mark or stamp of quality. Similarly we put a label or an *'ex-libris'* in our books, and we sew initials on sheets and handkerchiefs. Modern use of signs is so widespread and accepted that we can even be affected at a subliminal level. From this we can understand without difficulty a good number of biblical texts.

3. *Mark and sign in the Bible.* I would like to comment on some texts where the mark can signify

possession or in which it has a protective function. Job makes his plea and offers it to God saying, 'Here is my signature'. The High Priest wore a diadem with a precious stone on which was engraved 'Holy to the Lord' (Ex 28:36-37). Second Isaiah announces the restoration of the people and their belonging to the Lord:

Is 44:5 This one will say, 'I am the Lord's',
another will call himself by the name of Jacob,
and another will write on his hand, 'The Lord's',
and surname himself by the name of Israel.

As the owner impressed his name on the handle of the jar, so the Israelites marked on their arms the name of their Lord and master.

In the Song of Songs, the bride says passionately, 'Set me as a seal on your heart, as a seal upon your arm' (Song 8:6). She wishes to belong totally to the other, to remain with him without ever being separated. She does not ask that he sets his own name on his arm or in his heart, but 'set me', so that I may be completely yours. Elsewhere she phrased it differently: 'My beloved is mine and I am his'. It is the union of love, strong as death. He remains sealed by her, for ever.

The poet of the exile boldly applies the image to God. Jerusalem, the city which personifies the people, is the bride of the Lord. She laments that her bridegroom has forgotten her, and he protests: 'Behold, I have engraved you on the palm of my hand, your walls are always before me' (Is 49:16): as if he carried on his skin a plan of the city as an indelible reminder.

There is also a protective sign. 'The Lord placed on Cain a mark so that no one who met him would strike him' (Gen 4:15). This mark indicates that he is under the direct jurisdiction of the Lord, and that no one will be allowed to execute the murderer. Ezekiel develops the theme in a vision: 'For her sins Jerusalem is condemned', and the Lord sends out those who must execute the sentence. But let us read the texts:

Ez 9:1 Then he cried in my ears with a loud voice, saying, 'Draw near, you executioners of the city, each with his destroying weapon in his hand'.

2 And lo, six men came from the direction of the upper gate, which faces north, every man with his weapon for slaughter in his hand, and with them was a man clothed in linen, with a writing case at his side. And they went in and stood beside the bronze altar.

3 Now the glory of the God of Israel had gone up from the cherubim on which it rested to the threshold of the house; and he called to the man clothed in linen, who had the writing case at his side.

4 And the Lord said to him, 'Go through the city, through Jerusalem, and put a mark upon the foreheads of the men who sigh and groan over all the abominations that are committed in it'.

5 And to the others he said in my hearing, 'Pass through the city after him, and smite; your eye shall not spare, and you shall show no pity;

6 Slay old men outright, young men and maidens, little children and women, but touch no one upon whom is the mark. And begin at my sanctuary!'

The mark, in Hebrew, is called a *tau*, that is, the letter *tau* which in ancient times was written with two cruciform strokes. The scribe marks the *tau*, the cross, on the forehead; it is a sign that means, 'faithful to the Lord', by virtue of which those marked are saved from destruction. It is a clear guarantee which the executioners must respect. A similar kind of thing is the mark of blood on the lintels and posts of the doors, when the Destroyer passed through the roads of Egypt receiving the tribute of the first-born. Or it is like the scarlet ribbon on the window of Rahab's house backing onto the walls of Jericho, which served to save the whole family (Judg 2:18). The Book of Revelation picks up and transforms the scene from Ezekiel:

Rev 7:2 Then I saw another angel ascend from the rising of the sun, with the seal of the living God, and he called with a loud voice to the four angels who had been given power to harm earth and sea,
3 saying, 'Do not harm the earth or the sea or the trees, till we have sealed the servants of our God upon their foreheads'.
4 And I heard the number of the sealed, a hundred and forty-four thousand sealed, out of every tribe of the sons of Israel.

4. With the preceding texts we have passed from a general cultural context to the religious context of the Bible. A couple of times we have already found the name as a sign on the diadem of the priest and in the tatooing of the faithful of the Lord. The name can be the mark, or part of the mark; we recognize the car by this circle with three spokes, and also by its name, Mercedes. The son bears the name of the father from whom he is born: Ezekiel son of Buzi, Jeremiah son of Hilkiah. The temple bears the name of the Lord; the altars are dedicated by invoking the name of the Lord. The blessing is performed by 'imposition', invoking the name of the Lord on the community.

5. *The Christian context*. St Paul says that 'where there is a Christian, there is a new creation, a new humanity': there is a new beginning, a new belonging. The Christian is incorporated in Christ through

faith and remains sealed. Baptism is a sign, a life-giving mark which cannot be wiped out; this mark is nothing less than the mark of the Spirit, imposed by God; with it God sanctifies and consecrates. From this moment there is a new man, because he is a son of God; in being adopted he receives a share in the divine life, beginning to live with a new breath.

Eph 1:13 In him you also, who have heard the word of truth, the gospel of your salvation, and have believed in him, were sealed with the promised Holy Spirit,

14 which is the guarantee of our inheritance until we acquire possession of it, to the praise of his glory.

4.30 And do not grieve the Holy Spirit of God, in whom you were sealed for the day of redemption.

The birth to new life is expressed efficaciously in the symbol of water as the fruitful womb of the Church; as an action there is added the sign of the cross and the invocation or dedication to Father, Son and Holy Spirit. There we have both sign and name.

Here an important clarification is necessary, because the phrase 'in the name of' can be misunderstood. We have seen in Hebrew two examples of consecration to the Lord with the expression *'leYahweh'*, that is, the preposition *(le)* signifying offering or belonging and the personal name of God *(Yahweh)* (Ex 28:36 and Is 44:5). Other examples use the term 'name':

2 Sam 7:13 He shall build a house in my honour/for my name *(lismi)*.

1 Kings 7:13 A temple in honour of the name of the Lord *(lesem Yhwh)*.

Mal 1:11 They offer sacrifices and offerings to my name *(lismi)*.

However, to signify that one is acting 'in the name of another', as a representative of someone, Hebrew uses the preposition *be-*: Ex 5:23; Deut 18:20.22; 1 Sam 25:5-9; 1 Kings 22:16; Jer 20:9; etc. In the first group, the Greek translator uses the term in the dative: *to onomati;* in the second, he uses *en onomati.* The baptismal formula of Matthew 28:19 adopts an unequivocal expression of consecration: 'in the name...', *eis to onoma.* In modern language, when one acts or does something 'in the name', one is representing another person or being; but one does not use the expression 'consecrate, dedicate the name of N.', but simply 'dedicate to N.', unless one makes an exception of the phrase, 'put in the name of', as in transferring property. The baptismal formula, 'I baptize you in the name of the Father', could be interpreted in this way, as if the celebrant was performing 'as a representative' of the Father. The true meaning is that of a total dedication, a consecration, a putting in the name (into the possession) of the Holy Trinity.

6. So great is the sign of the cross and the trinitarian name placed on this creature that he begins to be 'super-man', a son of God sealed for ever. However our life is not only ontologically radical fact, the ultimate indestructible foundation, because we are conscience and freedom. Our deepest being develops and expresses itself through *actions*, small and great, daily and decisive, intimate and visible – actions of which we are aware, which we remember or which we forget. The human being is a unified and profound being that makes itself what it is in many different ways.

Through the fact of acting as a Christian, we can say that the whole activity of a person is marked.

But because we possess ourselves through reflective awareness, and own our actions through freedom, we must consciously mark all our works and all our activities, each and every day, with the mark and sign of the Christian. Everything profound that subsists in our being displays itself in any activity in which we engage, in the new day that dawns bringing to us the programme of our commitments, and perhaps some unforeseen pleasure. Then we sign with the cross this day, this journey, this action, in the name of the Father and of the Son and of the Holy Spirit.

We mark our activity and our rest, our joys and sorrows, with the sign of the cross and the trinitarian name, and in that way we fulfil our Christian being in the course of life. Even our death will be marked with the sign of the cross. Not that works and actions have need of a new consecration, when the deepest nucleus of existence is already consecrated by baptism; but with this act we add to every action the splendour of awareness, the dynamism of freedom.

What do we mean by 'marking' our activity with the sign of the cross? The cross means sacrifice for love, it is death for resurrection. The sign of the cross over our actions signifies to wipe away our selfishness and free us for love; it means renouncing what is empty, renouncing prestige and the longing to possess and to dominate, in order to consecrate the work to Christ. It is a sacrifice of self for a higher life. A work that is done through pure selfishness cannot carry the sign of the cross, it is not crucified; it is not sanctified in a Christian sense; an apostolic work, done for love of neighbour, is offered and consecrated.

Rom 14:7 None of us lives to himself and none of us dies to himself.

8 If we live, we live to the Lord, and if we die, we die to the Lord; so then, whether we live or whether we die, we are the Lord's.

To wipe out the selfish meaning of an action is to mark it with the cross; it is also to free it and make it available for a new dynamism, a trinitarian one. Here is the greatness and the responsibility of making oneself holy.

So when we begin the most important work of the week or of the day, when we begin the Eucharist, we sign ourselves in the name of the Father and of the Son and of the Holy Spirit. Thus the trinitarian meaning of the celebration of the Eucharist, which will come up again as the liturgy unfolds, is proclaimed from the very beginning.

2. THE PENITENTIAL LITURGY

1. When there is no particular reason to the contrary, our eucharistic celebration begins with a penitential liturgy, that is, a liturgical action in which the ministry of reconciliation takes place. At present this action is not a special form of the sacrament of penance; and I do not intend to discuss here the problem of its meaning and its original purpose. We can consider it as a 'sacramental', but something more than a beating of the breast and a taking of holy water. The ministry of reconciliation is abundant and generous on the part of God, and the Church can exercise it in different ways, according to the circumstances of time, place and persons. We would like to note such a penitential liturgy in a text of St Paul:

2 Cor 5:18 All this is from God, who through Christ reconciled us to himself and gave us the ministry of reconciliation,

19 that is, in Christ God was reconciling the world to himself, not counting their trespasses against them, and entrusting to us the message of reconciliation.

20 So we are ambassadors for Christ, God making his appeal through us.

Strictly speaking, we do not reconcile ourselves; it is God who reconciles us, and we 'let ourselves be reconciled' with him. The act implies the cancellation of a debt or the pardon of a sin, in order to re-establish good relations. This pardon is offered by God through Christ, and the Church must place itself at the service of reconciliation.

It is necessary to stress the interpersonal character of the act. We are speaking about a debt which affects two people, the debtor and the creditor; if we were speaking of an offence, it would be between the offender and the offended. Rather than infringing an objective norm, have we not failed in our duty to another person, a duty of justice or of love?

2. *Duties and deeds.* God takes part as the offended party and the people, the community, as the offending party. We do not deny that on other occasions God acts as Judge, in an exalted and impartial position, condemning the guilty and absolving the innocent. In the Old Testament there are numerous examples of this activity, specifically in the supplications of the accused and persecuted innocent person, and also in eschatological texts. However, these are not penitential liturgies aiming at reconciliation. In the penitential liturgy of the Old Testament, God is not a judge but an offended party. We can see that this is the case in many of the prophetic lawsuits, in Psalms 50-51 and in other penitential psalms.

The offended party wishes to re-establish good personal relations, and must do so not mechanically but in a personal way which involves the offender. One cannot say, 'It does not matter, I have forgotten all, nothing has happened', until the offender completes the process of transformation. If the offender has freely and consciously failed in his duties something serious has happened, and the offended person will not say, 'It's nothing really', because that would not be a responsible act of reconciliation between two persons. Instead, one would open up a dialogue, put forward a complaint and take legal proceedings so that the offender might recognize the fault and ask pardon for it. Only in that way can reciprocal personal relations be re-established.

If the offended person says that what happened does not matter, this implies that the offender is of no importance to him as a person. Every time that we despise the criticisms of rivals, we are thereby despising them as persons. For God, the offender matters as a person and therefore what has happened also matters to him. He wishes to cancel the debt, to remove the stain, to relieve the guilt and forgive the transgression, but he wishes to do so by involving the conscience and responsibility of the offender. Only at the end can he say: 'I have completely forgotten'. Responsibility means to respond – to someone, about something. For this reason the penitential liturgy is a legal process which includes a summons, a debate and a sentence. This process, which is the mystery of grace in action, takes the external form of a bilateral judgement deciding between two parties, the offending and the offended. The external form is like a drama which actually brings about what it represents. It does so through its so-called 'performative' expressions (the word *perform* means 'to put into effect'). When a president says: 'I declare the session open', it is really and juridically open and has legal validity. When the liturgical assembly represents a bilateral judgement of reconciliation between two opposing parties, what it represents is actually happening.

This process or efficacious representation normally develops in three stages: accusation, confession and pardon.

3. *First stage: accusation.* The offended party summons the offender, reminds him of his obligations and reproves his shortcomings. This stage is implicit and is not expressed in our penitential liturgy. It is implicit in the liturgical gathering. In the new Italian Missal we find an allusion to this:

> The Lord Jesus, who invites us to the table of the word and the eucharist, calls us to conversion.
> We are called to die to sin... .
> The Lord has said: let the one who has not sinned cast the first stone.

We will spare ourselves the reading and citation of all the relevant Old Testament passages; I will refer to just a few of them, taken from the psalms and the prophets:

Ps 50:6 God himself comes to the judgement.
7 Hear, O my people, and I will speak,
O Israel, I will testify against you.
21 These things you have done, am I to stay silent?
But now I rebuke you, and lay the charge before you.

Jer 2:5 What wrong did your fathers find in me
that they went far from me,
and went after worthlessness,
and became worthless?
8 The priests did not say, 'Where is the Lord?'
Those who handle the law did not know me;
The rulers transgressed against me;
The prophets prophesied by Baal.
13 For my people have committed two evils:
they have forsaken me, the fountain of living waters,
and hewed out cisterns for themselves,
broken cisterns
that can hold no water.

At this point it would be good to read and meditate upon the whole text of Jeremiah 2:1-4:4.

The accusation is based upon obligations which have been agreed, and it appeals to them. There exists, that is, a reciprocal obligation which has been spelt out in a series of clauses. This obligation is the Covenant, and the clauses are listed in the Covenant document. 'Gather to me my faithful ones who made a covenant with me by sacrifice' (Ps 50:5). 'What right have you to recite my statutes or take my covenant on your lips?' (Ps 50:16). The Sinai Covenant sets out ten clauses; in Greek *deka-logoi*, the Decalogue; the document was inscribed on a tablet of stone which was preserved in the temple. Because of these clauses God could lodge a complaint against his people, since they had not fulfilled the duties which they had solemnly undertaken. The people with one voice had promised, 'What the Lord has said, we will do!' (Ex 19:8; 24:3.7). For the community gathered to celebrate the Eucharist what is the point of reference? Is it always the Decalogue of Sinai? The Sabbath precept and the prohibition against making images of God are no longer in force; the remainder continue to have value to some degree, even if not in their original sense. The Christian does not live in the old covenant, but in the new. The protocol of the new covenant is not the Sinai Decalogue but the Gospel of Christ. The Beatitudes, or Sermon on the Mount, or the precept to pardon one's enemies do not form part of the Decalogue; and where it retains its validity it has been profoundly transformed. It is not correct to say that the basis of the Christian life as regards behaviour is the Decalogue. In chapter 5 of Matthew we read statements like the following: 'You have learned that it was said to the elders... but I say to you... It is also commanded... but I say to you...'. Instead of

Moses as mediator there is Jesus, the Messiah, the Son of the Father; in place of Sinai, there is the mountain in Galilee; in place of the ten precepts or prohibitions there are eight beatitudes; instead of tablets of stone, the Spirit in the heart. From this centre there are organized the other demands, norms and counsels of the gospel which are concentrated in the double love of God and neighbour. It is clear that the Gospel includes and deepens whatever is permanent in the Decalogue, whereas the Decalogue does not contain the whole gospel.

However, this gospel accuses us in many ways. It is our commitment to God the Father, through the mediation of his Son. Do we carry it out, and to what extent? The Gospel is a joyful announcement, good news; is it not also an act of accusation against us? We could read a page of the Gospel taking it as complaint by the Lord against his own. Does this Christian community really believe that sharing is a value? Or does it continue to believe that acquiring and possessing is a value? Does this Christian community believe that it is a value and a requirement to work for peace? Is it preoccupied with a problem of this nature? Does this community feel a thirst for justice? Readings and reflections of this type would allow the biblical message to cut into the Christian community with greater efficacy.

The Gospel summons us, accuses us, and then offers us pardon and reconciles us. For this reason we used to say '*Per evangelica dicta deleantur nostra delicta*', 'through the words of the gospel may our sins be blotted out', not in a mechanical way, but in a responsible way, within a process of call and response.

I have already said that this stage is barely

touched upon in the penitential liturgy in our celebration of the Eucharist. Furthermore, there are occasions on which another liturgical or paraliturgical act takes precedence, such as the recitation of Lauds, when the whole of the penitential rite is omitted. Other occasions, when we can carry it out with greater leisure and calm, will help us penetrate the meaning of this part of the Mass.

4. *Second stage: confession.* The accused and criticized party could defend itself, denying the facts or the charges. But when it is God who reproves our conduct how can we deny it? 'How can you say "I am not defiled"? Why do you complain against me? You have all rebelled against me' (Jer 2:23.29). In this case it only remains for us to confess the fault and ask pardon.

We are accustomed to prepare for this by leaving a space for silence, so that those present may specifically call to mind their more important or more recent faults, or those faults that are strictly to do with the particular celebration. A few words can guide the reflection. Then the guilty party recognizes its fault and asks pardon of the offended party.

The Old Testament offers us innumerable examples of this second stage:

Ps 32:5 I said, 'I will confess my transgressions to the Lord'.
Ps 38:5 For my iniquities have gone over my head;
they weigh like a burden too heavy for me.
Ps 51:1 According to thy abundant mercy blot out my sin.
2 Wash me thoroughly from my iniquity
3 For I know my transgressions,
and my sin is ever before me.
Ps 65:3 When our transgressions prevail over us
thou dost forgive them.

Ps 130:3 If thou, O Lord, shouldst mark iniquities,
Lord, who could stand?
4 But there is forgiveness with thee,
that thou mayest be feared.
Jer 3:22 Return, O faithless sons,
I will heal your faithlessness.
Behold, we come to thee;
for thou art the Lord our God.
25 Let us lie down in our shame,
and let our dishonour cover us;
for we have sinned against the Lord our God.

The Missal offers us two formulae: 'Lord, have mercy on us, for we have sinned against you' and 'You came to call sinners, Christ have mercy'. In the new Italian Missal there are formulae which are richer and more developed:

> We recognize that we are sinners and trustingly we invoke the mercy of God.
> Humble and penitent like the publican in the temple, let us approach the Holy and Just God, that he may have mercy on us sinners.
> Christ, who on the cross prayed for pardon for sinners, have mercy upon us.

Let us note another important aspect. In the penitential liturgy of the Mass it is not isolated individuals who are acting, it is not something that takes place between individuals and God. It is not that we are all meeting by chance in the same place and that we all say the same words together in order to save time. The individual dimension is not totally ruled out, but it is not the main one in this case. It is true that the *Confiteor* is spoken in the first person singular: 'I confess to almighty God and to you, my brothers and sisters, that I have sinned...'. But even such a formula, recited in the singular, is shared with a reciprocal effect of confession and witness of the 'brothers'. Characteristic of the penitential liturgy in the Eucharist is its communitarian aspect. Beyond the unrenounceable individual responsibilities, there is a solidarity in guilt. The two elements neither oppose nor exclude one another, even if at times it is difficult to harmonize and integrate them. There are some who fear that by emphasizing the communitarian responsibility we may want to weaken personal responsibility or actually do so; however, this is not so.

The Old Testament offers us some communitarian confessions of sin after the Exile, precisely at the time when Ezekiel has reaffirmed individual responsibility (Ez 18). An eloquent example that picks up and amplifies what we have said is Baruch 1:15-3:8, from which we quote a few verses:

> 1:15-18 And you shall say: 'Righteousness belongs to the Lord our God, but confusion of face, as at this day, to us, to the men of Judah, to the inhabitants of Jerusalem, and to our kings and our prince_ and our priests and our prophets and our fathers, because we have sinned before the Lord, and have disobeyed him, and have not heeded the voice of the Lord our God, to walk in the statutes of the Lord which he set before us'.
>
> 3:1 O Lord Almighty, God of Israel, the soul in anguish and the wearied spirit cry out to thee.
>
> 2 Hear, O Lord, and have mercy, for we have sinned before thee.
>
> 5 Remember not the iniquities of our fathers, but in this crisis remember thy power and thy name.

The responsibility belongs to the whole community, including even their ancestors. Each person considers himself to be one with the others in bearing the weight of the people's history. It is wonderful: united in the confession of a common sin, the scattered people feel themselves to be one. In the presence of God their sins do not suffocate the community, but unify it.

Even when Daniel prays in the first person singular, 'Hear the prayers and supplications of your servant', he does so in the name of all the people: 'The whole of Israel has broken your law, in refusing to obey you... Through our sins and our failures Jerusalem and the whole people are an object of shame. But even if we have rebelled, the Lord understands and pardons' (Dan 9). We could also read Ezra chapter 9 and Nehemiah chapter 9.

Co-responsibility is not opposed to individual responsibility; rather it includes it. The two elements can be developed in a simultaneous and harmonious manner, knowing that as individuals and as a community we are responsible before God. Not only does the individual Christian fail in his obligations towards the covenant, but so does this Christian community, as a community, fail in its evangelical commitment to Jesus Christ. The eucharistic penitential liturgy can be a suitable moment to educate and to strengthen this knowledge. Again the Italian Missal offers us suitable material:

> At the beginning of this eucharistic celebration, we ask for conversion of heart, the source of reconciliation and of communion with God and our brethren.
> Let us recognize that we are all sinners, and let us ask pardon of one another from the depth of our heart.
> Lord, you build us up as living stones to form the holy temple of God, have mercy on us.

5. *Third stage: pardon*. Even this stage is announced in plural form, and it is pronounced in the

form of a petition. God does not come as a judge to condemn the self-confessed sinner; he comes as the offended party to reconcile humanity with himself. The individual person cannot reconcile himself with God on his own initiative; nor does God have to reconcile himself with the human being. The action is that of God the Father and of Jesus Christ; 'Jesus Christ the just (innocent), intercedes for us and reconciles us to the Father' (from the new Italian Missal).

The final act of the bilateral judgement between the two parties can take place in three ways. Either the offender-debtor makes restitution or totally satisfies the offended person, and so the right relationship between the two is re-established. Or there is some form of arrangement or settlement: the offended person accepts partial compensation, a modest reparation, and states himself satisfied, while the offender makes amends for his wrongdoing and is accepted once again. Or the offended party renounces his rights, and pardons completely the debts and all the offences. It is up to the offended party to choose the outcome of the process; the offending party can only make supplication. The eucharistic penitential liturgy enters into the third form of resolution: God does the pardoning, and will seal the reconciliation with the banquet.

The president of the liturgical action adopts a form of supplication rather than an assertive form. He says, 'May almighty God have mercy on us, forgive us our sins, and bring us to everlasting life'. He does not say 'I forgive you', or 'God forgives us', but makes supplication, including himself among the sinful community, using the words "We, our". History tells us that in other ages, and in other regions of the Church, there was a supplicatory formula with sacramental validity (I will return to this matter on another occasion). Moreover, our present formula is quite ancient, or is based on ancient and traditional texts. Is it then a simple supplication? Does it not have in any way a 'performative', efficacious value? It is not performative in the sense that it realizes what it expresses, given that it does not announce anything; it is efficacious in so far as it has the guarantee that the petition will be heard, even if not in a sacramental form.

At this moment it is not God who speaks, nor even Christ, as who interceded from the Cross: 'Father, forgive them'. The priest does not speak as a representative of God, or of Jesus Christ, since he includes himself among the sinners. He speaks, as a full member of the community, in its name. But he speaks with the commitment and promise of the pardon of God, with the guarantee of the reconciliation effected through the Messiah: 'God has reconciled us with himself through Christ, and has entrusted to us the ministry of reconciliation' (2 Cor 5:18).

3. LITURGY OF THE WORD (I)

Those of us who are getting on in years, whose life has lasted for a couple of generations, can with a little mental effort remember the time when the Mass was 'The Sunday Obligation'. Moral theologians used to say that to fulfil the obligation without falling into grave sin it was sufficient to arrive at the Creed or the Offertory. Over a long period of time this custom had created a particular mentality. The Mass was a law, a precept, and the grave obligation was quantified. The first part, the penitential liturgy and the liturgy of the word with the homily, was less important, and so one could more easily dispense with it.

On the other hand, the readings in Latin could not be understood and the homily was not always strictly connected with the Gospel reading. To counter this situation there began a liturgical movement which inculcated the importance of the Eucharist in the Christian life and succeeded in distributing thousands and millions of translations of the missal. These were a suitable way of countering the prevailing liturgical practice.

We who had our backs to the congregation and understood the Latin texts, knew about the frequent repetition of some biblical texts – the commons of confessors, doctors, of a martyr, a virgin, of a non-martyr, or a non-virgin, of the dead...

I am referring to the fact that practice often shapes and reinforces a mentality no less than does theory. Another effect of this practice was the division of the Eucharist into two relatively autonomous, or at least separable, parts so that the true and proper Eucharist began with the Offertory.

1. What I have said so far is no more than an introduction, a background against which to expound our subject which is the Liturgy of the Word. I do not recall that in those days we used the expression 'Liturgy of the Word'. The new way of speaking came from a different theological vision which wanted to foster a new mentality. I believe that the formula has now taken root, though at what level I do not know. Along with the expression came some concrete reforms. The Second Vatican Council, in the Constitution on the Sacred Liturgy, put them thus:

> 24 Sacred Scripture is of paramount importance in the celebration of the liturgy.
>
> 35 In sacred celebrations there is to be more reading from Scripture, and it is to be more varied and suitable.
>
> 36 Since the use of the vernacular may be of great advantage to the people, the limits of its employment may be extended, especially in the readings and directives.

The texts quoted refer to the liturgy in general; the following quotation refers to the Eucharist in particular.

> 51 The treasures of the Bible are to be opened up more lavishly, so that richer fare may be provided for the faithful at the table of God's Word. In this way a more representative portion of the holy Scriptures will be read to the people over a set cycle of years.

In fact, much of the reform has already happened. Liturgical texts have been translated, and the repertoire has been enormously increased. On Sundays there are three readings instead of two, which has its advantages, although there are also some disadvantages. The advantage is that throughout the three cycles the Gospels are read almost entirely, along with a good part of the epistles and a notable amount from the Old Testament. Another advantage is that we see the connection between the Old and New Testaments. The disadvantages can be that the second reading does not fit easily into the theme, that the three readings must be short so as not to take too long and that one cannot possibly comment on all three.

The fact that the readings are read and proclaimed in the language of the people has produced, along with other factors, a notable change in the style of preaching. Today it is more homiletic, more at the service of the Biblical text. The liturgical readings and the homily have influenced to a great extent the renewed interest in the word of God.

2. The observations just made are external manifestations, symptoms or results of a principle and of a profound change. The principle is the fundamental unity of the eucharistic celebration, integrated by two components. One table only for the banquet, but two loaves, or one loaf in two forms; the bread of the word and the bread of the Eucharist. Nobody would say that H_2 is more important than O in water; 'sister water' is not a juxtapositioning, nor a mixing: it is a combining of hydrogen and oxygen. We should not think of the eucharistic celebration as a juxtaposing of parts, because it is a unity.

56 The two parts which, in a certain sense, go to make up the Mass, namely, the liturgy of the word

> and the Eucharistic liturgy, are so closely connected with each other that they form but one single act of worship (*Sacrosanctum Concilium*, 56).

This does not prevent the 'participation in the sacrifice' through communion being the culminating moment (n. 55). There is no value in laying this down in terms of legal obligation, nor in calculating the limits of such an obligation. The important thing is the reform in understanding and practice. To remove the liturgy of the word from the eucharistic celebration is not to separate two parts, but to mutilate an organism.

It is this unity, composed and articulated, and the relationship between its parts, which I am now about to explain.

3. I have used the Conciliar formula 'the bread of the word'. Now, for pedagogic reasons, I would like to distinguish between word and bread. Consequently, we must reflect in these pages on the liturgy of the word and the liturgy of bread. Word means Word of God, Sacred Scripture. Bread will mean specifically the bread which is the Body of Christ. I listen and I feast.

Consecrated bread and word. But why so many words? Are we not satiated with words? 'Love is doing rather than speaking.' Will not so much talking just produce word inflation? Will not such insistence on the 'liturgy of the word' make the word of God engender exhaustion? From a different point of view, others object or comment: 'Why is it so important? This passage from St Paul to the Romans, even though it is read in contemporary language, I still don't understand it. At best I accept it meekly, but without any conviction.'

On the other hand, even in our culture we are tired of words and demand deeds. There is a proverb which says, 'It's one thing to preach, another to give bread', and in the words of a song, 'In the house and in the temple, for every child of Adam, one sermon needs no example, and that's to give one's bread'. We do not hunger for words, but for bread.

To counter these quotations I find in the Gospels some words of Christ. I think of a polemical encounter between Christ and Satan, the opponent of the Father's plan. Responding to Jesus' hunger for bread Satan says: 'Tell these stones to become bread'. Jesus replies, 'Not by bread alone does one live, but by every word that comes from the mouth of God' (Mt 4:3-4). It is a citation from Deuteronomy (8:3) which explains how God had educated his people in the desert, as a father educates his son:

> Deut 8:3 And he humbled you and let you hunger and fed you with manna... that he might make you know that man does not live by bread alone, but by everything that proceeds out of the mouth of the Lord.

What proceeds from the mouth of God is his word, in particular, 'the commandments of the Lord your God' (Deut 8:6). The life of the Israelites as a people depends, it is true, on material food, but far more it depends on the word of God.

Here we find two teachings opposed to one another. Popular wisdom tells us that words are not enough, that deeds are required, whereas the wisdom of the gospel tells us that bread is not enough, that words are required. Which shall we accept?

4. Words are not enough, it is true, but if these words are words of God... Even though they are

composed by human beings and pronounced by them, they carry the breath of God and can give us life.

A word of commandment is one 'by doing which one will live' (Lev 18:5). A word is that which reveals to us who we are, and it exposes our illusions. A word is that which denounces and exhorts, threatens and promises; words in which God communicates himself, and communicates his life. 'Lord, to whom shall we go? You have the words of eternal life', says Peter to Jesus after the discourse on the bread of life (Jn 6:68).

Words are not enough. But if these words are words that God addresses to human beings, the Word which comes from him and becomes man and lives in human form... Made man, he continues to be fully Word; both when he speaks and when he keeps silence, when he works miracles and when he suffers without working any. The Word is he who always speaks to us, because in him everything is word; who 'in the beginning was with God' (Jn 1:1), and then became a man of weak flesh like ours, and pitched his tent among us.

'One does not live by bread alone.' To be sure, bread does not give life; it only preserves and prolongs it. We burn it in small portions, and with the energy of this combustion we move and we run. During our lifetime we use some of it to grow and fortify ourselves. With its calories bread prolongs life, but it does not guarantee it. It does not insure us against fire, accident or illness. Our daily bread is a ration to help us live one day longer; to go on a little further. At one stage it contributes to a life in growth; later it sustains a life in decline. We do not live by bread alone.

If however this bread is the word of life, if it is the form in which the glorified Son of God really gives himself to us, then we live by bread. This is because this bread introduces and develops in us a life that has no end, if we do not destroy it; a life that will pass beyond the river of death. Indeed, it is by the glorified Christ made bread, by the word made food, that we live.

The Word concentrates in himself many words. He is the *verbum abbreviatum* of which many ancient authors spoke: a succinct word, that says many things; a word that summarizes, like the pithy title of a large book. 'God, who had already spoken in ancient times in many and different ways to our fathers through the prophets, finally, in these days, has spoken to us through the Son' (Heb 1:1-2). Since this word summarizes and concentrates all the words of Scripture, these words develop and articulate, they refract into many colours, and break into many facets the one and definitive Word. This Word, which one day took human form, and is now glorified, hides itself in the eucharistic bread. In the form of food, it communicates its life to us. Before we receive this bread, so tiny yet so immense, white and mysterious, a few words can explain to us some aspect of its mystery. The Mystery of Christ was manifested in a few years of life, in a certain number of teachings, in a few specific miracles. Although John tells us: 'There are many other things which Jesus did. Were every one of them to be written, I suppose that the world itself could not contain the books that would be written' (Jn 21:25). Only one part of the mystery succeeds in manifesting itself, and it does so in a concentrated manner. To unravel the hidden mystery, the liturgy uses the Gospels, and along with them the texts of the Old Testament: preparation, prophecy, symbols that it exposes to the light of the New Testament. When they are illuminated by this light, they explain aspects of the mystery. Just as a folded carpet must be unfolded to show the design, in the same way a symbol mentioned or alluded to by the Gospel explains its meaning by means of its corresponding image in the Old Testament, if we interpret it and correctly bring it to light. The whole purpose of the Liturgy of the Word is to illuminate for us the mystery of Christ – what it represents for us, what it offers us, what it demands of us.

In this way the words of the eucharistic liturgy are truly 'words of life' and are an integral part of the eucharistic celebration.

5. During the Second Vatican Council, a representative of an Eastern Church briefly expounded the thought of many orientals about the inspired word. From the intervention of Mgr Edelby I would like to take up and comment on a text which will help us to understand our present subject. I will comment on a few phrases:

> Scripture is a liturgical and prophetic reality; a proclamation rather than a book; the testimony of the Holy Spirit in the Christ event, whose privileged moment is the eucharistic liturgy. Through this testimony of the Spirit, the entire economy of the Word reveals the Father. The post-Tridentine controversy has seen in Scripture first of all a written norm. The Eastern Churches see in it *the consecration of the history of salvation under the species of the human word, inseparable from the eucharistic consecration, which recapitulates the whole of history in the body of Christ.*

Let us take note of the centrality of the eucharist and the union of the two consecrations: a history under the species of the word, a body which recapitulates the history under the species of bread and wine. To explain the 'consecration of history under the species of the word', I turn to the text of Luke on the annunciation: 'The Holy Spirit will come upon you, and the power of the Most High will overshadow you. He who will be born will be holy and called Son of God' (Lk 1:35). Since the conception took place under the shadow of God the Father through the intervention of the Holy Spirit, this man who now begins to exist is from the first instant consecrated. He is Son of God. These are no titles or privileges which are added later.

Something similar happens when, through the impulse of the Spirit, an episode of human history becomes word. If there exists escapist literature, there also exist great literary works such as myths and legends, epic and story, drama and lyric poetry. Through these texts we sometimes communicate with the poet who expresses himself in them, at other times we communicate with a human experience which can be individual or general. The great story-tellers and playwrights one day feel that in their mind has been conceived a personality, possibly historical or legendary, possibly purely fictional. They begin by creating and developing a character, so that little by little it acquires a life of its own which the author must respect. These characters represent and incarnate important human experiences. At other times the great anxieties, distresses and hopes of human beings pass into the mind of the poet and are transformed into poetic language. The great works of literature offer us a vicarious experience which enriches us as human beings. In our way we relive it, or join with the characters and their deeds. It all comes to us in the form of poetic language, simply human.

Up to a certain point it is the same with the Bible. One anonymous author narrates a scene from patriarchal life, another recounts the epic of liberation, another sings of the hope of returning to the homeland. The experience of a few personalities and a people is transformed into a permanent word. But here is added something qualitatively different and superior, because this transformation is accomplished through the impulse of the Spirit. What results, the word, emerges consecrated; it is the Word of God.

Let us take as an example the crossing of the Red Sea. A community lives the experience of liberation, overcoming enormous obstacles, under the guidance of a charismatic leader who operates in the name of God. An author, or different successive authors, give the experience the form of literature, in epic tone, with legendary elements and symbols that perhaps have a mythical origin. Through this text successive generations communicate with the original experience. What is more important, they also communicate with their God, the Lord who communicates himself to them. For if it was God who guided the great crossing, it was the Spirit who moved the writer. Centuries later, an Israelite grievously suffered from being abandoned by God. In a crisis of faith, he searches in vain for a reply to his question:

Ps 77:7 Will the Lord spurn for ever,
and never again be favourable?
8 Has his steadfast love forever ceased?
Are his promises at an end for all time?
9 Has God forgotten to be gracious?
Has he in anger shut up his compassion?

Until suddenly there arises in his mind the memory. In his fantasy he sees before him the vision of the crossing of the Red Sea which he knows through having read and heard the traditional texts. The vision acquires such a force that it is as if he himself were taking part in it, as if he and his generation had joined themselves to the great march and had contemplated the theophany of God. Now, in serenity, he distances himself and transforms his experience into lyrical language:

Ps 77:18 The crash of thy thunder was in the whirlwind;
thy lightnings lighted up the world;
the earth trembled and shook.
19 Thy way was through the sea,
thy path through the great waters;
yet thy footprints were unseen.
20 Thou didst lead thy people like a flock
by the hand of Moses and Aaron.

Centuries later, we turn to read or hear the story of the crossing of the Red Sea during the Easter Liturgy. And once again we communicate with the ancient experience through a text that is 'consecrated' and inspired. The text shows its meaning, which is the revelation of the liberating God; only this time the first liberation refers to that definitive revelation which is the Passover of Christ. In our liturgical proclamation the Spirit breathes again and the words ring out as inspired. Therefore this consecration must not be separated from the other.

6. There is another history of salvation concentrated in Jesus Christ. It is the story of humanity, its joys and its pains, its illusions and its disillusions, its greatness and its smallness. All of this is concentrated in a special way in specific co-ordinates of

time and space in this man, Jesus of Nazareth, a Jew, born of woman, born under the law. His life is like the concise synthesis of human life, right up to death, since he did not wish to renounce the final and definitive human experience, which is to die. Being raised by the Father, all this experience was glorified. His birth is not abolished, it remains glorified; his miracles have not passed away, they persist in glory. His words, recalled by memory and placed in the Gospels, are more meaningful because they are glorified.

Now he wishes to communicate with us his glorified experience, his life with its meaning, the meaning of life. How will he communicate it so that we can assimilate it? By consecrating his glorified life under the species of bread and wine. In the eucharistic banquet we communicate with the historical experience and the glorified life of Jesus Christ. We do not separate this consecration from the other, the consecration under the species of the word.

When the biblical texts are read, may the Holy Spirit who lives in us enable us to listen and attune our hearts to the words of Scripture. May the inspired word be able to resound within us, inspiring us; may it fill us with the wind of the Spirit. May the whole community resound in harmony. Through the words of Scripture may the whole community communicate with the word of God, and with Christ who is his Word.

> The Church has always venerated the divine Scriptures just as she venerates the body of the Lord, never failing, especially in the sacred liturgy, to nourish herself from the bread of life from the table of the word of God and the Body of Christ (*Dei Verbum*, 21).

4. LITURGY OF THE WORD (II)

1. It is a common phenomenon in many religions to find the liturgy composed of words and gestures. One school of research expresses this by speaking of 'myth and ritual'. The gestures – or ceremonies or rites – are made up of positions, movements and actions. We call them gestures because they usually have a natural or conventional meaning. Sometimes the gestures are organized in a kind of mime or dramatic action, with words to accompany and explain it.

It is good for us to start with the myth. This narrates with symbols a primordial deed which becomes the foundation for periodic rhythms, for example the cycle of vegetation. The myths often include divinities among their characters, but this is not essential. It is normal to use symbolic language, created out of elementary symbols. The story that one tells when reciting a myth can be dramatized or stylized in a representation which is ritual.

We do not find divine myths in the Old Testament. The biblical authors do not avoid symbols of mythical origin, but they know how to apprehend them and purify them in order to exploit the striking impression that they make. Usually the Old Testament has transmitted historical or legendary narratives, prayers and rituals as separate entities; therefore it is not easy to combine them correctly in order to reconstruct its liturgies. Nevertheless, we can find a few significant examples. The ceremony of the offering of first-fruits in Deuteronomy 26 is well known. It was celebrated in local sanctuaries and it commemorated in the gift of the annual harvest the fundamental gift of the land. The people responded to the gift of the harvest with the little symbolic gift of the first-fruits, and to the gift of the land with the recital or confession of their history under the guidance of God. (Note that in Hebrew to offer means 'to make enter, to introduce' and harvest means 'entrance, crop' – that which one puts into the granary or cellar.) Though the text is well known, it seems opportune to read it again here.

Deut 26:1-11 When you *come into* the land which the Lord your God gives you for an inheritance, and have taken possession of it, and live in it, you shall take some of the first of all the fruit of the ground, which you *harvest* from your land that the Lord your God gives you, and you shall put it in a basket, and *you shall go* to the place which the Lord your God will choose, to make his name to dwell there. And *you shall go* to the priest who is in office at the time, and say to him, 'I declare this day to the Lord your God that *I have come into* the land which the Lord swore to our fathers to give us'. Then the priest shall take the basket from your hand, and set it down before the altar of the Lord your God. And you shall make response before the Lord your God, 'A wandering Aramaean was my father; and he went down into Egypt and sojourned there, few in number; and there he became a nation, great, mighty, and populous. And the Egyptians treated us harshly, and afflicted us, and laid upon us hard bondage. Then we cried to the Lord the God of our fathers, and the Lord heard our voice, and saw our affliction, our toil and our oppression; and the Lord brought us out of Egypt with a mighty hand and an outstretched arm, with great terror, with signs and wonders; and *he brought* us into this place and gave us this land, a land flowing with milk and honey. And behold, now *I bring* the first of the fruit of the

> ground, which thou, O Lord, hast given me'. And you shall set it down before the Lord your God, and worship before the Lord your God; and you shall rejoice in all the good which the Lord your God has given to you and to your house, you, and the Levite, and the sojourner who is among you.

The ceremony is simple and meaningful. It is the people who give it its meaning. It is not derived from a magic rite. It requires a small sacrifice of the first of the produce, the best and choicest, and with it goes a profession of faith. Those social groups who do not possess land – the Levite and the immigrant – must also participate in the festival. The social dimension is founded upon the religious. Can a similar ritual be deprived of meaning?

If we take away the great profession of faith, the ceremony is diminished, even if it does not lose all its meaning. If we pass over the great references to history, the rite threatens to fall into ritualism without any explicit meaning. From there it is easy to pass on to an act of magic for ensuring the new crop. If we leave out the participation of the needy classes, the rite remains lifeless, because it would be set at the service of egoism and deny the God who is liberator of the oppressed and protector of the disinherited. A similar loss of meaning can be called 'ritualization'; the rite becomes 'ritualism'.

2. Israel repeatedly succumbed to the danger of ritualization. In one way or another, the rites and the whole liturgical act lose their significance. So those who are present no longer 'participate', they simply assist, like the deaf man who does not hear, like the stranger who does not understand the texts and their interpretation, like a non-believer who assists out of courtesy, or for social reasons. The

whole celebration, with its words and gestures, becomes closed in on itself, and far from putting people into relationship with God it locks them into an empty ceremony. The people, including the cultic professional, carry out the celebration, correctly keeping to the traditional ways, but empty it of meaning closing it in itself, and in that process enclosing all inside. Is there a way out?

One senses the need for an external and superior appeal, for a power which is not just at anyone's beck and call, for someone who from outside can open a breach in the closed and vicious circle. It is the prophetic word, the ultimate appeal in Israel, above king, priests and judges. The Jews believed that by possessing the temple in Jerusalem the city was protected against every danger. Whatever might be their conduct, or their perversion, the temple would look after them. On one occasion in the same temple, in the presence of the people gathered together, Baruch read this denunciation in the name of Jeremiah:

> 7:8 Behold, you trust in deceptive words to no avail.
> 9 Will you steal, murder, commit adultery, swear falsely, burn incense to Baal, and go after other gods that you have not known,
> 10 and then come and stand before me in this house, which is called by my name, and say, 'We are delivered!' — only to go on doing all these abominations?
> 4 Do not trust in these deceptive words: 'This is the temple of the Lord, the temple of the Lord, the temple of the Lord'.

The prophet does not condemn the cult, but a cult which has become so perverted. Isaiah calls it 'useless offerings, abominable incense... I cannot endure iniquity and solemn assembly' (Is 1:13). If the liturgy is not a circle of presence and of contact with the divinity, the circle must be broken from without and a breach opened in the wall of indulgence and complacency. Since those within who are responsible do not do it, the prophet must do it from without, firing like an arrow the word of God. Through this means sovereigns and priests come to fear the resounding of this word, as powerful as the trumpets of Jericho, and seek to condemn the prophet, as happened to Jeremiah (Jer 26), or to banish him, as was the case with Amos. In the name of king Jeroboam, the priest Amasiah threatened the prophet Amos:

> 7:12 O seer, go, flee away to the land of Judah, and eat bread there, and prophesy there;
> 13 but never again prophesy at Bethel, for it is the king's sanctuary, and it is a temple of the kingdom.

King and priest are in agreement. The sanctuary is royal and national. In its sacred environment the word of God must not resound. In such a way they forcibly close the liturgical space to the message of God. But this message must resound, because God is sovereign, and cannot tolerate the perverting of sacred actions and places.

3. Let us come now to our own liturgy. This too is usually made up of words and ritual actions such as entrance procession, bows, genuflections, times for sitting or standing, and other actions, because both are combined in the course of the eucharist. If we say that in the Liturgy of the Word the word prevails over action, in the Eucharistic Liturgy both are there in equilibrium; the priest elevates the host and chalice, breaks the host, distributes communion.

So do we too run the risk of ritualizing our celebrations? We cannot avoid the risk, and so it is useful to know it and to confront it. The danger is to ritualize the whole ceremony and in particular the Liturgy of the Word. In the Old Testament the prophetic word was external to the rite, it acted upon it or against its distortion. It was a sovereign invasion of the cultic space. I would describe the phenomenon as like a circle where an arrow pierces the surface. We have incorporated the word of God as a component part of the eucharistic celebration. The arrow stands within. Will it shoot against someone or something? The danger now is the transformation of the biblical readings into just one more rite, removing the sting from the word. We listen barely opening our ears. We say, 'This is the word of the Lord', and we have got through another ceremony. This would be to blunt the sharp sword of the prophet or evangelical word.

It would be a refined perversion or a fatal omission to domesticate liturgically the word which challenges the community. The biblical word must preserve its full force. Although it is within, it must be heard as if it came from without, breaking through and penetrating, as if meeting us head on, confronting us and shaking us. The Israelites said to Moses, 'You speak to us, and we will listen, but let not God speak to us, lest we die' (Ex 20:19). We say, 'Let Christ speak to us, and we will live, let Christ speak to us and we will live as Christians'.

4. The opposite of ritualization is the acceptance of the word with faith, inasmuch as it is a word which is inspired or full of the Spirit. It is acceptance and then digestion, as one digests food – the bread of the word – or it is like an appliance which is

plugged into the electricity supply and receives energy with which to function. It is in this way that we must imagine and understand the biblical word in the celebration. It is active and dynamic, in the form of language.

What I mean to say is that it does not work in a magic way, like an unintelligible incantation, an *abracadabra*. Rather it works through perception and understanding. It follows therefore that it is important to proclaim the texts in a language which the assembly understands, and it is profitable to explain them and comment upon them in the homily. I am speaking of the spiritual comprehension of the free person who is not closed to the voice of the Spirit. When the listeners jeered at the prophet, imitating his oracles, Isaiah replied in the name of God, 'With stuttering lips and an alien tongue he will speak to this people' (Is 28:11). Ezekiel proclaims it with greater clarity:

> 3:4 Son of man, go, get you to the house of Israel, and speak with my words to them.
> 5 For you are not sent to a people of foreign speech and a hard language, but to the house of Israel.
> 6 — not to many peoples of foreign speech and a hard language, whose words you cannot understand. Surely, if I sent you to such, they would listen to you.
> 7 But the house of Israel will not listen to you: for they are not willing to listen to me.

When we have a spiritual understanding, the word does not simply convey information, but communicates power.

The prophet of the exile, Deutero-Isaiah, offers us a classic text. To turn his compatriots to hope, he has nothing but words. He cannot confirm them with signs. But they are the words of God, and their confirmation will take place when those who were living in hope make their return to their homeland a reality. So the prophet puts his preaching within the framework of two declarations on the power of the word. In the first chapter of his message he opposes the word of God to humankind. He juxtaposes the wind and the word of God. Men and women are grass, and their plans wither and fade. These plans stir around in the human mind without assuming a definite form. Yet how many assume form without coming to fruition! Humankind is grass and their plans are straw, especially when these plans contrast with the plan of God. Because then the breath of God, which can give life, causes them to wither. However, the plan of God become word will fulfil itself in due time. The exiles can build their hope on the foundation of the promise.

> Is 40:7 The grass withers, the flower fades,
> when the breath of the Lord blows upon it.
> 8 The grass withers, the flower fades;
> but the word of our God will always be fulfilled.

At the end of his message the prophet develops the concept with an image of fertility. I have spoken of the energy of the word; it would be better to speak of its fruitfulness. Referring back to the old symbol which imagined the dew and the rain as heavenly seed which fertilizes Mother Earth with vegetation, the prophet describes the activity of this word which comes down from heaven and embodies itself in human language, coming with a mission or a task in history.

> Is 55:10 For as the rain and the snow come down from heaven,
> and return not thither but water the earth,
> making it bring forth and sprout,

giving seed to the sower and bread to the eater,
11 so shall my word be that goes forth from my mouth;
it shall not return to me empty,
but it shall accomplish that which I purpose,
and prosper in the thing for which I sent it.

The appearance of bread in this context is interesting. The ultimate mission of the rain is to give humankind bread for this year and the seed for sowing next year. The Liturgy of the Word has in view the eucharistic bread, which is the Word sent from heaven. In the parable of the sower the word is compared with seed (Mt 13:18-23).

Fruitfulness is not the same as efficaciousness. The fruitfulness of the biblical word has its rhythms. If on the one hand we should await concrete results from the readings of the Mass, on the other hand we cannot impose on them our measure of time and intensity. Yes, we must hope that the words will accomplish their mission.

> The force and power in the word of God is so great that it remains the support and energy of the Church, the strength of faith for her sons, the food of the soul, the pure and perennial source of spiritual life. Consequently, these words are perfectly applicable to sacred Scripture: "For the word of God is living and efficient" (Heb 4:12) and is "able to build up and give the inheritance among all the sanctified" (Acts 20:32) (*Dei Verbum* 21).

The mission of the word of God is to ensure that the Church penetrates the Mystery of Christ. It is a mystery like an ocean, inexhaustible, concealing all the treasures of wisdom (Col 2:3). It is the task of the Spirit to 'teach us everything' and 'lead us to all truth' (Jn 16:13). One of its privileged instruments is the inspired word.

5. In the eucharistic celebration the Liturgy of the Word is the privileged moment for reading and listening to Scripture. From this centre other readings extend – paraliturgies, group reading and private reading – and towards it they also converge. 'In all the brooks of Judah the waters will flow, a river will flow from the house of the Lord' (Joel 4:18 [Hebrew]). Scripture is the source of life, situated in the temple, in the celebration rather than in the enclosure. From it spring up and flow rivers which irrigate all the regions of the Church. The Christian not only drinks from this source in the Mass, but from it derives an irrigation canal. If they continue with the reading and let it overflow through contemplation, one day they will find a clear deep lake within themselves in which heaven is reflected:

Sir 24:30 I went forth like a canal from a river
and like a water channel into a garden.
31 I said, 'I will water my orchard
and drench my garden plot';
and lo, my canal became a river,
and my river became a lake.

From this lake they can communicate to others: 'The teaching of the wise is the fountain of life' (Prov 13:14). 'The mouth of the righteous is the fountain of life' (Prov 10:11). We can apply this to the wisdom and prudence of the Gospel which the Christian has also assimilated by means of Scripture. Then we will say of him, with good reason: "the words of a man's mouth are deep waters" (Prov 18:4).

For this reason the Constitution *Dei Verbum* recommends the reading of the Bible, especially in the liturgy:

> Therefore, all the clergy must hold fast to the sacred scriptures through diligent sacred reading and careful study, especially the priests of Christ and others, such as deacons and catechists, who are legitimately active in the minstry of the word. This cultivation of Scripture is required lest any of them become 'an empty preacher of the word of God outwardly, who is not a listener to it inwardly' since they must share the abundant wealth of the divine word with the faithful committed to them, especially in the sacred liturgy. This sacred Synod earnestly and specifically urges all the Christian faithful, too, especially religious, to learn by frequent reading of the divine Scriptures the 'excelling knowledge of Jesus Christ' (Phil 3:8). 'For ignorance of the Scriptures is ignorance of Christ'. Therefore, they should gladly put themselves in touch with the sacred text itself, whether it be through the liturgy, rich in the divine word, or through devotional reading, or through other means suitable to the purpose (*Dei Verbum*, 25).

The experience of only twenty years, a mere couple of hours in the history of the Church, teaches and confirms that the Liturgy of the Word in the eucharistic celebration is a nucleus that reaches out in a dynamic way. It provokes other gatherings with all their consequences. It is not surprising that with the decline in reading the Bible among Catholics, especially in Latin countries, that the Liturgy of the Word in the eucharistic celebration had lost practical importance. In recovering the ancient tradition which perhaps had been weakened because of the post-Tridentine polemics, the reading of the Bible and the Liturgy of the Word simultaneously recover their privileged position.

In this way, therefore, through the reading and study of the sacred books, let 'the word of the Lord run and be glorified' (2 Thess 3:1) and let the treasure of revelation entrusted to the Church increasingly fill the hearts of men and women. Just as the life of the Church grows through persistent participation in the Eucharistic mystery, so may we hope for a new surge of spiritual vitality from intensified veneration for God's word, which 'lasts forever' (Is 40:8; 1 Pt 1:23-25) (*Dei Verbum*, Conclusion).

5. OFFERTORY – EUCHARIST – BERAKA

I am now going to explain the part we call the Offertory, which signifies or denotes the offering of gifts. I will explain this action by developing it in two directions: first, by going back to biblical practices and expressions, and secondly, by commenting on the present text of the Offertory, even if that means I have to move into other parts of the Mass.

The present text reads:

> Blessed are you, Lord God of all creation. Through your goodness we have this bread/wine to offer, which earth has given and human hands have made/fruit of the vine and work of human hands. It will become for us the bread of life/our spiritual drink.
>
> [*Latin:* Benedictus es, Domine, Deus universi, quia de tua largitate accepimus panem/vinum, quem/quod tibi offerimus, fructum terrae/fructum vitis et operis manuum hominum, ex quo nobis fiet panis vitae/potus spiritalis.]

Sometimes the Offertory is carried out by first taking the bread and wine in procession to the altar. At other times it is limited to the action of the priest in elevating the gifts. On some occasions other gifts may accompany the bread and wine.

The text is a beautiful synthesis of the celebration which in Greek we call *eucharisteia*, in English *thanksgiving*, in Hebrew *beraka*. I will begin with a leisurely exposition of the Hebrew term.

1. *Beraka.* An historical exposition would have to study Jewish liturgical forms in order to trace their influence and development in the Christian formulae. This study has been done by specialists. In Spanish we for example have a learned study by J.M. Sanchez Caro, *Eucaristía y historia de la salvación.* My aim is more modest, and more tied to the Old Testament. Perhaps this will allow me to make a useful contribution, at least for meditation.

It is well known that the Jewish liturgy uses some 'thanksgiving' formulae called *beraka,* or *birkat* which were distinguished according to the time during the meal when they were used. *Beraka* is therefore a formula; its Christian equivalent is the *anaphora.* But in the Old Testament *beraka* means something more; it also signifies the gift.

The Hebrew root *brk,* especially *barek* in the *piel* conjugation, is usually translated 'to bless', but it is necessary to nuance the translation. Basically the verb assumes two people, and something good in respect of one of them. The blessing of A refers to something good with respect to B. If B does not possess it, the blessing is a wish that he/she might obtain it. If he/she already has it, the purpose is to congratulate them for it. For example a friend tells us that he/she is going to take an exam or enter a competition. We wish him/her good luck, and a happy outcome. In so doing, we are 'blessing' them, which means, literally, we are 'speaking well' of them. Later on we meet them, and they tell us that they have been successful. Then we show our delight with them. Both these ideas are contained in the verb *brk,* according to the occasion.

There is a Hebrew proverb which says:'To say "Good Morning" at dawn with a loud voice is like uttering a curse'. To greet someone with a 'Good Morning' is also *brk*, to wish them to have a good day. To say 'Good Morning' goes back to an old expression which when complete went like this 'Good Morning to you/to us from God'. It is to desire something good for the other for the whole day, to 'bless' them. In English we can wish someone 'All the best' while the Germans say '*alles Gute*'. These formulae can degenerate into simple greetings of courtesy through social convention. Genesis 47:10 and Exodus 12:32 seem to refer to such a greeting on the occasion of a departure. The sense of congratulating someone for the achievement of something good is clear enough in 2 Samuel 8:10: 'He sent to King David his son Joram to greet him and to congratulate him *(brk)* because he had waged war against Hadad-Ezer and had beaten him'.

When the other person has done us a favour, our blessing is rather more of a 'thanksgiving'. We bless = we say 'Thank you'. With this we enter into our new terrain, for which it will be useful to cite a few examples:

Deut 24:12	If he is a poor man, when the sun goes down you shall restore to him the pledge that he may sleep in his cloak and bless you.
Job 31:19	If I have seen any one perish for lack of clothing, or a poor man without covering;
20	if his loins have not blessed *(brk)* me, and if he was not warmed with the fleece of my sheep...
2 Sam 14:22	Joab fell on his face to the ground, and did obeisance, and blessed the king.

There is a final step in human relations. The thanksgiving/blessing can accompany the words with a gift or present that expresses the feeling of gratitude. It is not a payment which equals the benefit received, it is the tangible expression of gratitude. It must be something significant, not mean, in accordance with the means of the person who has received the gift. Jacob had stolen from his elder brother Esau his father's last blessing, and the brother swore vengeance. Jacob emigrates, and after many years decides to return to his father's home, but he must cross the territory controlled by his brother. In order to ingratiate himself, he adopts a humble and generous attitude, sending before him more than 400 choice animals. 'He was thinking: I may appease him with the gift that goes before me, and afterwards I shall see his face; perhaps he will accept me' (Gen 32:21). At last the two brothers meet, and Esau asks:

Gen 33:8 'What do you mean by all this company which I met?' Jacob answered, 'To find favour in the sight of my lord'.

9 But Esau said, 'I have enough, my brother; keep what you have for yourself'.

10 Jacob said, 'No, I pray you, if I have found favour in your sight, then accept my present from my hand; for truly to see your face is like seeing the face of God, with such favour have you received me.

11 Accept, I pray you, my gift that is brought to you, because God has dealt graciously with me, and because I have enough'.[1]

The stolen blessing *(beraka)* of his father (Gen 27) is compensated by the new present *(beraka)*.

The daughter-in-law of Caleb approaches him and says to him, 'Give me a present' *(beraka)* (Josh 15:19). When Naaman is healed he returns to give thanks to Elisha: 'Accept a gift from your servant'

[1] See the commentary in my book: *¿Dónde está tu hermano? Textos de fraternidad en el Génesis,* Valencia 1985, pp. 213-215.

(2 Kings 5:15). A generous man is called *nepesh beraka* (Prov 11:25). Job receives 'the blessing of a vagabond' (*beraka* = thanksgiving) (Job 29:13).

2. Now that we have established this important point I can introduce a third person to the stage, namely God. He has already appeared implicitly, because when the poor person approached and 'blessed' his benefactor, he was wishing on him God's blessing, and in wishing him well he was referring to God as the giver. This scheme has a triangular shape: the beneficiary, in order to give thanks, invokes on his benefactor the divine blessing: 'Blessed are you by God for the good you have done to me'. We recall the Christian expression, 'May God reward you'. It is as if to say, 'I wish you great good, so great that I cannot give it. The only thing I can do is to ask God to reward you for your goodness'.

The entry of God into the scheme of thanksgiving complicates it but at the same time enriches it. There arises a double relationship. I, the one benefited, wish good to my benefactor, and ask God that he may give him good so as to repay him on my behalf. The two things are not exclusive, but rather complementary. I cannot make a greater gift to this person than to desire that God should compensate him. If I should succeed in having God reward him, there is no thanksgiving to equal it. For this the Hebrew would say, 'May you be blessed by God, for...'. When Abram returned from his victory in which he freed the prisoners, the king-priest of Salem blessed him:

Gen 14:19 Blessed be Abram by God most High,
maker of heaven and earth

20 and blessed be God most High,
who has delivered your enemies into your hand.

With this let us pass to the final section. Once again it has a double aspect which puts humankind in relation with God. When the subject of the verb is God, the word is action, it is efficacious. God blesses the person with fruitfulness (Gen 1:28); he blesses the works of humankind (Job 1:10), the growth of the field (Ps 65:11), the bread and water (Ex 23:25), the dwelling place (Prov 3:33), the patriarchs (Gen 12:2; 22:17; 25:11), the people (Deut 1:11; 14:24). 'To bless' (or 'to say well') for God means 'to do good', to 'bene-fit'.

To the benefits of God, the human being responds by blessing God. At this point the verb carries another meaning. Human beings can neither do good to nor wish well to the supreme Good. At most they can congratulate him for the good that he possesses. They can also recognize the benefits they have received and give thanks for them. This act is like a free offering of themselves. In Hebrew the word *barek* is used for 'to bless' in this sense. The Book of Psalms uses the verb *brk* in this sense more than twenty times.

There is a psalm which illustrates quite well and concisely the alternating movement between the human blessing God and God blessing the human. This is Psalm 134, which I will keep for the final reflection, since our Eucharist ends with a blessing.

There remains just one element – the gift which accompanies the words. Can we offer God a gift? Strictly speaking, we can give nothing to God. All we express with the gift is our thanksgiving. The offering of the first-fruits (Deut 26), that I have already mentioned, is a good example, but it does not use the word to bless. In Hebrew cultic offerings are called *minha* (which in the profane sense means 'tribute'); they are not called *beraka*. They would serve us well to explain the term 'offertory'. Now, my intention is to explain the offertory as eucharist = *beraka*, commenting on the whole formula. Having said this, I believe that we can provide a mental context which allows us to advance without becoming disorientated.

3. I will stay with the gifts understood as *beraka*, in the Old Testament sense. The Eucharist or thanksgiving is not just verbal, but is materialized in the offering of some gifts. The text begins like this: 'Blessed are you, Lord, God of all creation. Through your goodness we have this bread/this wine'. Why do we use the title 'God of all creation'? We bring just a little bread and wine, so why such a broad and solemn invocation?

Because it is in the humble that the sublime is revealed. Because we choose a gift that in its smallness is a compendium of manifold immense gifts. We have made this bread round and white in colour, as if to signify by the roundness totality, fullness and perfection, while the colour white is the synthesis of all the colours. Even if it had another form and another colour, the important thing is that it is 'fruit of the earth': 'which earth has given'. So, in bread the earth is present, fertile mother earth. With her fertility she feeds her children. Blessed are you, Lord, for the gift of the earth! For millions of years you have prepared it so that it might be a dwelling place for your children. There is no bread without an earth which receives the seed in its womb. She also receives the rain, through which bread is the fruit of the earthly and heavenly water. The rain paternally fertilizes the maternal earth. Blessed are you, Lord, for the rain which makes the young shoots grow! Bread is also the fruit of heaven, that is, of the atmosphere where the water arose before descending again. And how could it rise, overcoming its weight, concentrating and moving itself through the air, until it broke down into millions of drops with which it irrigates the soil centimetre by centimetre? A force has lifted it, mightier than the force of gravity - the sun with its heat. Blessed are you, Lord, for the might of the sun!

The sun – which belongs to a system which centres and balances the planets, and incorporates constellations and galaxies. The stars – which rotate and maintain themselves in a mobile and prodigious equilibrium, never ceasing, never tiring. Each has its place, exerting the exact and precise force so that the earth can duly receive rain and can produce its fruit. Bread, fruit of earth and water, wind and stars. Fruit of the light, which activates the working of chlorophyll, and of alternating darkness, which guarantees its vitality. Fruit of the regular rythmn, pulse of earthly time, systole and diastole of the heart of our system. Blessed are you, Lord, for the light which is concentrated within this bread, which is reflected on its white surface! Fruit of the earth, with its forces both physical and chemical, its roots which suckle the sap, its pressure which strengthens the stems, its silent, hidden activity. The plant harbours within itself forces which oppose one another in co-ordination – the force which pushes the roots downwards, overcoming the resistance of the minerals, the force which pushes upwards, overcoming gravity. How can the tiny tender shoot open a way through the compact barrier of soil, breaking and separating the sod, with an inexorable push upward until it reaches its exact height? Bread, fruit of the plant, of the earth and its multiple forces. Fruit of the earth means time and rhythm too, because the grain does not germinate suddenly, in a moment. It must rely on the brief pulse of night and day, as also on the slow rhythm of the seasons; the cold silence of winter, the surprising re-awakening of the spring, the growing heat of summer. It is all necessary, so that this piece of bread may come to be. For its sake the earth must rotate, gently inclined in its orbit, approaching and distancing itself from the sun in exact measure. Blessed are you, Lord, for this bread, fruit of the earth and of the seasons! And we have not yet finished, because this bread, this harvest is the fruit of a seed taken from the harvest in the previous year, 'so that it may give seed to the sower and bread to eat' (Is 55:10). This was the fruit of another preceding year, and so we must go back through the centuries, through the millennia, without interruption. This bread which we offer you today embraces one process of thousands of years and opens up to another, with a little human history and a lot of natural cycles.

This piece of bread means much, and so we offer it as a gift, small and condensed. We account for it by means of causes, physical and chemical, along with elements and stars. Behind all this and in all this we discover you, Lord of all creation, like a solicitous father of a family who works the fields to give bread to his own.

Ps 65:9 Thou visitest the earth and waterest it,
thou greatly enrichest it;

the river of God is full of water...
for so thou hast prepared the earth.

10 Thou waterest its furrows abundantly,
settling its ridges
softening it with showers,
and blessing its growth.

11 Thou crownest the year with thy bounty
the tracks of thy chariot drip with fatness[2].

Through your goodness we have this bread/wine to offer. [Latin: *De tua largitate accepimus panem/vinum quem/quod tibi offerimus.*] Such words should serve as a concentrated expression of our amazement and our gratitude.

4. We offer it to you Lord, because it is ours, it is the fruit of human work, 'the work of human hands'. Many people have collaborated in making this piece of bread, according to the division of tasks which our culture imposes. At other times, and perhaps even in other places, a man or a family were able to bring the grain from the seed to the point where it left the oven. Today it is not so. If we were able to unravel the threads of activity converging on this centre, we might perhaps find more than a thousand: farmers who sow and harvest, mechanics who use and repair machines, transporters, bakers, shopkeepers. At every stage there is a group working together. This human work is not cursed. You, O Lord, have blessed it, and through it 'we go out to our work, to our toil until the evening' (Ps 104:23). Today, physical work is more endurable; the sweat of the brow has been transformed, almost to the point of disappearing. But the toil and the perseverance have not disappeared. We

---

[2] See the commentary in my book: *Treinta Salmos. Poesia y oración*, Madrid 1986, 2nd ed., pp. 261-263.

can add the intellectual labour of many people. Once upon a time someone invented domestic cultivation, a Noah of wheat, of maize or of rice. Another discovered how to extract and work iron; many others perfected it. Someone else invented the plough. Much later on other sources of energy were discovered: petrol for cars, electricity for ovens. Other machines were invented for different purposes. How many necessary inventions all converge and come together in the narrow circle of this piece of bread. It is the fruit of human work, and as such we offer it.

It is human work, and for this reason it does not amount to mere physical labour or mental effort; it embraces humankind in its daily existence. Work means the sustaining of oneself and one's family; it also means the occupation which gives meaning to one's life. How painful it is to remain without work; with the tedium of not knowing what to do, the frustration of feeling useless, the pain of not being able to earn enough. One works for an ideal, for a dream; for the family, for society. Work gives life to a person as a social being. His specific work moves in a constellation of many different yet complementary kinds of work. It is not just slavery, it is also freedom and nobility. Or it is both together, heaviness and lightness like the elastic which stretches and relaxes. Bread is the fruit of manifold human work – of many human beings and many aspects of work. Therefore we offer it to you, as our very own.

It is true that you have given it to us: 'Through your goodness we have this bread/wine'. You gave us the earth, but the earth would not give bread without human work, which is our own. You gave us the strength to work, the intelligence to invent, the skill to organize, and the love to justify the effort. It is simple, but it is ours, and with it we can express our thanks to you. It is true that we cannot enrich you, and that you have need of nothing. But we can offer you our thanks and our gratitude. It is a thanksgiving which does not humiliate but exalts, because it allows us to raise ourselves to you with our gifts. Receive this our bread, it is our eucharist, our *beraka:* From your goodness we have received it and now we present it to you.

6. EUCHARIST - BERAKA

1. 'Blessed are you, Lord, God of all creation. Through your goodness we have this wine to offer. Fruit of the vine and work of human hands'. We could repeat here what was said about bread, since wine too is a universe in microcosm which reveals the Lord of creation to me. The Old Testament presents us with a legend about the origin of wine. It was invented by Noah after the Flood. The story tells us two things which refer to our situation. In the first place, wine is double-edged, because it gives joy and removes sound judgement. Secondly, wine, or the vine, inaugurates decisive stages: the time after the Flood, the entry to the promised land which displays its fruit in the form of an enormous bunch of grapes, the era of Christ, inaugurated in his person, in the light of the heavenly consummation. In the case of the eucharistic wine there is no ambiguity, unless we think of the 'sober inebriation' of which one liturgical hymn speaks. A new era begins, that of the new promised land in which we live. So in what sense does the wine strip us and leave us defenceless?[1]

The story of Noah leaves out the stages in the preparation of the wine. It mentions only the work of cultivating the vine. We can think of that time of silence or murmuring during the fermentation. The must lies in the darkness, while a myriad of bacteria

---

[1] See the commentary in my book: *¿Dónde está tu hermano? Textos de fraternidad en el Génesis,* Valencia 1985, pp. 48-49.

works within it transforming the sugar into alcohol. Fruit of the earth, through the mediation of the vine; fruit of the vine, through the mediation of micro organisms or chemical substances. Silent activity is even present in the wine. It too is a gift of God and becomes our gift.

Perhaps human work, with its inventiveness and tenacity, is more obvious in wine than in bread. There are many kinds of soil, so that human activity takes different forms. There are many wines, different in aroma and taste. In their variety, we offer them as a polyphony of tastes, as a multicoloured palette of aromas. And we put no ban on it, as did the Nazirites (Num 6) or the Rechabites (Jer 35).

2. Why bread and wine? Could we not have chosen different elements, for example first-fruits (Deut 26)? What do bread and wine mean for us? For many, over the course of millennia, bread has been the basic food. There are cultures which make bread from maize, and others which eat rice without transforming it into bread. In our language we use the expression 'earning one's bread', which is equivalent to earning one's living, because bread is equivalent to food.

Bread is, or means, the basic food of human beings. It is the food which sustains our life day by day. In being broken down it renews us and permits us to work. It is transformed into part of us or into life-giving energy. If bread is the fruit of human work, human work is the fruit of bread. Bread either is or signifies the elementary basis of our nourishment, even if in reality it is not everything. Humankind has invented many other foods, even making cooking into an art, the culinary art. All the same, bread remains what it basically is. It is not refined, or exotic, or costly, but simple and accessible. When it is rationed, there is pressing need; when it is lacking, there is hunger:

Is 30:20 And though the Lord give you the bread of adversity and the water of affliction.

Jer 37:21 So King Zedekiah gave orders, and they committed Jeremiah to the court of the guard; and a loaf of bread was given him daily from the bakers' street, until all the bread of the city was gone.

38:9 Jeremiah will die there of hunger, for there is no bread left in the city.

52:6 The famine was so severe in the city, that there was no food for the people of the land.

Bread is humble and simple. It is unassuming. It gives itself without resistance. In this generous humility we concentrate the expression of our thanksgiving to God. I would say that it is our daily 'prose'.

Whereas wine is our 'poetry', our enjoyment, our festivity, bread and water are the indispensables. 'Indispensable to life are water, bread, clothes and a house to live in' (Sir 29:28). To fugitives one offers what is most necessary: 'Go to the thirsty and bring water... give the fugitives bread' (Is 21:14).

But when one honours someone and gives them a feast, one offers bread and wine, which is equivalent to a lavish meal, a banquet. When the Israelites say, 'They ate and drank', they mean wine (Judg 19:4). Ben Sirach counts among the essentials of life 'wheat, flour and blood of the grape' along with milk and honey, oil and salt, and these are meant for a life that is not simply survival. If to the fugitive is offered bread and water, to the victor returning from battle 'Melchizedek, king of Salem, offered bread and wine and blessed him' (Gen 14:18).

Wine is a pleasure, a 'perk' that we add to food. Wine is also simple and noble, and can be full of meaning. As a pleasure, it represents the useless aspect of life, that which gives meaning to life, without which life would not be worth the trouble. The useless can be more important than the useful. So wine represents the poetry alongside the prose. It is like colour compared with a world of black and white. It is like music compared with sounds and noises. It is like dancing compared with walking. It is playing compared with working. It is the art and craft compared to simple technique. It is the humorous as opposed to the serious: 'What is the life of those who have no wine, for wine was created at the beginning to make us glad' (Sir 31:27).

Wine is joy: 'Their heart shall be glad, as if drunk with wine' (Zech 10:7); 'You make the food of the earth grow, and wine to gladden the human heart' (Ps 104:14-15); 'Joy of the heart and joy of the soul is wine drunk duly and in moderation' (Sir 31:28); 'Wine and music gladden the heart, but more again does love make it glad' (Sir 40:20)

The last text suggests that wine is friendship and love. 'A new friend is like a new wine, when it is aged you will drink it with pleasure' (Sir 9:15). Wine has more flavour when it is shared. It is the brother of love, as the Song of Songs keeps repeating:

1:2 Your love is better than wine.
4 We will extol your love more than wine.
2:4 He has taken me to his wine cellar.
4:10 How much better is your love than wine.
7:10 Your palate is like the best wine.
8:2 I would give you spiced wine to drink.

Because it signifies love and has the colour of blood, it also represents sacrifice, especially sacrifice done out of love. Three times the Old Testament refers to wine as 'the blood of the grape' (Gen 49:11; Deut 32:14; Sir 39:26). We remember the undertaking of the three heroes of David, who risked their lives and sacrificed themselves to comply with a wish, or perhaps a whim, on the part of their leader:

2 Sam 23:14 David was then in the stronghold; and the garrison of the Philistines was then at Bethlehem.

15 And David said longingly, 'O that some one would give me water to drink from the well of Bethlehem which is by the gate!'

16 Then the three mighty men broke through the camp of the Philistines, and drew water out of the well of Bethlehem which was by the gate, and took and brought it to David. But he would not drink of it; he poured it out to the Lord,

17 and said, 'Far be it from me, O Lord, that I should do this. Shall I drink the blood of the men who went at the risk of their lives?' Therefore he would not drink it.

Wine, signifying love and sacrifice, is suggestive of the mysterious relationship that exists in human beings between love and sacrifice. Love is not authentic if it refuses self-sacrifice. A sacrifice has no value unless it is born of love.

Because wine is also gladness it reveals to us the joy and satisfaction of self-sacrifice for love. It is a paradox that human beings can delight in that for which they suffer, but love resolves the paradox. Wine is joy, it is sacrifice, it is love; it is the joy of sacrifice out of love. Finally, wine derives from the transformation of sweetness into alcohol or spirit. It enters our blood stream as a new spirit or feeling, as a dynamism which liberates and encourages, as long as we take it in moderation. All this is the meaning of wine.

So, bread and wine is what we offer you, Lord. You have chosen them, simple and humble, yet loaded with meaning. You have taught us to bring them together to your table. You have given them to us in your goodness, and now we present them to you. 'Blessed are you, Lord, God of all creation: through your goodness we have this bread to offer, which earth has given and human hands have made' and this wine, 'fruit of the vine and work of human hands...', and now 'we present them to you'.

Strictly speaking, I really should end here my explanation of the Eucharist as thanksgiving, as *beraka*. But the liturgical formula adds and anticipates two essential elements: consecration and communion. I could leave them to their proper place, which would be more logical. I can comment on them here, which will be more coherent. Because in a certain way the liturgical text is a complete symphony. By treating the rest of the formula here, I will give my exposition the key to unite the principal elements.

4. The liturgical text continues, 'It will become for us the bread of life', 'It will become our spiritual drink'.

We prepare the table by laying the tablecloth, lighting the candles, adding flowers, along with a plate for the bread and a cup for the wine. We do not need much. To this banquet in miniature we invite no less a person than God. The Book of Judges gives two naive stories about two men who invite the Lord, or 'the angel of the Lord' (his manifestation or his messenger). One of these is Gideon.

Judg 6:17 'If now I have found favour with thee, then show me a sign that it is thou who speakest with me.

18 Do not depart from here, I pray thee, until I come to thee, and bring out my present, and set it before thee'. And he said, 'I will stay till you return'.

19 So Gideon went into his house and prepared a kid, and unleavened cakes from an ephah of flour; the meat he put in a basket, and the broth he put in a pot, and brought them to him under the oak and presented them.

20 And the angel of God said to him,'Take the meat and the unleavened cakes, and put them on this rock, and pour the broth over them'. And he did so.

21 Then the angel of the Lord reached out the tip of the staff that was in his hand, and touched the meat and the unleavened cakes; and there sprang up fire from the rock and consumed the flesh and the unleavened cakes; and the angel of the Lord vanished from his sight.

It is as if the Lord had eaten the banquet that was offered by means of the fire which is his minister. Slightly different is the case of Manoah, the father of Samson:

Judg 13:15 'Pray, let us detain you, and prepare a kid for you.'

16 And the angel of the Lord said to Manoah, 'If you detain me, I will not eat of your food; but if you make ready a burnt offering, then offer it to the Lord'.

19 So Manoah took the kid with the cereal offering, and offered it upon the rock to the Lord, to him who works wonders.

20 And when the flame went up toward heaven from the altar, the angel of the Lord ascended in the flame of the altar while Manoah and his wife looked on; and they fell on their faces to the ground.

In the temple, as well as the sacrifices there was a more simple offering, namely, the twelve 'loaves of the presence', offered every week to the Lord.

So, we invite him to our table, and he accepts the invitation, but in such a way as to reverse the roles so that he invites us, transforming our bread and our wine. 'Bread for bread and wine for wine', says the proverb. But in the present case it is not so, because bread and wine are signs. God takes the bread and transforms it into the glorified body of his Son, so that his glorified life may be communicated to us in the form of food. Jesus, who has given his life for us, now wishes to give his life to us, a new and indestructible life. It is a fairly simple way of communicating life; the food we take in vivifies and vitalizes us. The bread which we chew, swallow and digest is 'unmade' in order to 'make' us. In other words, we assimilate it.

Part of it is incorporated in our tissues, part is burned and produces energy. We can speak of matter and energy when we consume food. While we are consuming it, it is consuming itself, and we continue to live and function. Jesus was first 'unmade', broken down in his passion and consumed by death. Now glorified, he does not need to be broken down in order to give himself; he simply takes the sign of food, that is bread. He does not give a fragment of provisional and temporary life, condemned to die, but establishes and furthers a life which will overcome biological death. 'It will become for us the bread of life.'

Jn 6:47 He who believes in me has eternal life...
48 I am the bread of life.
49 Your fathers ate the manna in the wilderness, and they died.
50 This is the bread which comes down from heaven, that a man may eat of it and not die.
51 I am the living bread which came down from heaven; if anyone eats of this bread, he will live

> for ever; and the bread which I shall give for the life of the world is my flesh.

In the same way, God accepts the wine and transforms it into the glorified blood of his Son; the blood which was shed in the passion is now alive. That blood is the sacrifice for love; bleeding out of love and with joy. He offers it to us in the form of drink. It is not the blood of vengeance of which Zechariah spoke: 'They will devour the slingers like flesh, they will drink their blood like wine' (Zech 9:15). Nor is it the blood of vindictive justice which Isaiah describes: 'Why is your garment red, and your inhabitants like one who treads the winepress. I have trodden the winepress alone, and none of my people were with me. I have trodden them in my indignation, I have trampled them in my wrath. Their blood is sprinkled upon my garments, and I have stained all my raiment' (Is 63:2-3). It is quite the opposite. With meekness, and without anger, he let himself be trampled on and crushed. He was bathed with blood. He shed all his blood out of love. It is not the blood of eschatological judgement that Joel announced: 'Take up the sickle, for the harvest is ripe. Come and trample, for the winepress is full' (Joel 4:13). It is blood shed to make us alive, to give life. It is given to us to drink in the form of wine… 'It will become our spiritual drink of salvation.'

So the Father accepts our humble gifts, to change them into exalted ones. Wheat is ground down, as Christ was ground down, made into bread and delivered to men and women to be unmade in giving life, as Christ was fully delivered for men and women, and returns to deliver himself having been made bread. Must is trampled from grapes, as Christ was trampled and changed into wine to ease our thirst and restore us, as Christ bled and returns to deliver himself to us having been made wine, to ease our unquenchable thirst to be and to live.

5. From its many grains the wheat forms a cake to be shared out among the whole Christ, as Christ, who is the unity of all humanity, is shared out among all. The trampled fermented grapes have become wine, to strengthen a blood bond, to experience the intoxication of love. Thus Christ offers himself in the Eucharist, and thus we receive him: 'It will become for us the bread of life', 'our spiritual drink'.

But here comes the decisive difference. When a person eats bread and drinks wine, they assimilate it. When a person receives the glorified body and blood of Christ, it is Christ who assimilates himself to them, uniting them in himself. In dividing himself among many, he wishes to make all into a new body, a 'Christian' community. Pay attention to that adjective. Christ assimilates himself to us by making himself man, then he assimilates us to himself making us Christian. Giving us his blood to drink, he makes us his blood relations and establishes a new blood circulation in his body which is the Church. We should feel this blood beating in the organism of the Church.

In a similar way every Christian must be assimilated, must become like Christ. They must appear to Christ as bread, that is, they must learn to be better than bread; they must learn to share and give of themselves. What they have, and what they have received, they must share out and divide – space in hospitality, time in service, talents in deeds. Thus they will be good Christians, bread divided for the community. They must make themselves like Christ as wine, relying on the joy of sharing with those who weep, infecting them with good humour. Intoxicated with the Spirit of Christ, they must live with fraternal love, so that all are brothers and sisters 'in blood'. They must learn the meaning and value of sacrifice as the seal of love and the source of life.

'Blessed are you, Lord, God of all creation. Through your goodness we have this bread to offer, which earth has given and human hands have made. It will become for us the bread of life... Blessed are you Lord, God of all creation. Through your goodness we have this wine to offer, fruit of the vine and work of human hands. It will become our spiritual drink.'

7. EPICLESIS

1. The word *epiclesis* is a Greek noun which derives from the verb *epikaleo* (to call, invoke). In the technical sense, it means an invocation to God the Father or to God the Holy Spirit. In the exposition that follows our interest is particularly in the action of the Spirit. We can invoke the Father, that he may send the Spirit, or we can invoke the Spirit, that he may come. We invoke him with regard to an action which is above our capacity, and which belongs to God alone.

We normally say that the priest 'consecrates', but we must be careful not to use the expression misleadingly. No one would claim that a man, even as a priest, could be the efficient cause which transforms bread and wine into the body and blood of Christ. The priest is a minister, and through his ministry God himself is at work. Moreover, the priest is a minister inasmuch as he is a full member of the Church. A naive interpretation could leave us with a 'magic' conception of the sacramental or eucharistic action.

There was once a debate, even a controversy, about the authentic formula of sacramental action. Should one say, 'I absolve you', or 'May the Lord absolve you, may he pardon you'? Similarly, should one say, 'This is the body of Christ', or 'May the Lord transform this element into the body of Christ'? Now, since in the Eucharist we normally find two formulae, one in narrative form, 'this is...', and the other an invocation, 'that this may become...', the controversy can be expressed in other ways. Which of the two is the formula that consecrates, which one is essential and which secondary? This controversy divided the Churches of East and West. The Eastern Churches defended the invocation or *epiclesis*, while the Western Churches supported the narrative or *anamnesis*. The two linguistic forms, of announcement or of petition, summed up two theological visions.

Controversies sometimes help to clarify theological points and deepen our understanding of the mystery, but they can also degenerate into polemic, creating rigid opposing positions and making each side forget an aspect of the reality. I would like to use the controversy simply to introduce the topic, because among us it is not often that we comment or meditate on a fundamental aspect of the Eucharist. In the books we cited and recommended at the beginning, the reader can find much richer information and more profound discussion. Sanchez Caro alerts us to the apparent absence of 'anamnesis' or spoken narrative in some liturgies (cf. eg. p. 137); Gesteira offers us an excellent exposition, starting on p. 596.[1]

In the new Eucharistic Prayers, the epiclesis is more explicit and clearer than in the former Tridentine prayer. I will try to illuminate it with some passsages from the Old Testament.

2. *Ezekiel and the Spirit.* No text is so developed and evocative as the vision of a prophet during the exile. Life during the exile in Babylon and the return to the homeland are rooted in the extreme opposition between life and death. Death is almost a min-

[1] J.M. Sánchez Caro, *Eucaristía y historia de la salvación*, Madrid 1983; M. Gesteira Garza, *La Eucaristía, misterio de comunión*, Madrid 1983.

eral with its dry bones, the life of the spirit is dynamic and life-giving. By order of God the prophet must implore and pray for the Spirit. Let us read again the text, which is quite well known:

Ez 37:1-10 The hand of the Lord was upon me, and he brought me out by the Spirit of the Lord, and set me down in the midst of the valley; it was full of bones. And he led me round among them; and behold, there were very many upon the valley; and lo, they were very dry.
And he said to me: 'Son of man, can these bones live?' And I answered, 'O Lord God, thou knowest'.
Again he said to me, 'Prophesy to these bones, and say to them, O dry bones, hear the word of the Lord. Thus says the Lord God to these bones: Behold, I will cause breath to enter you, and you shall live. And I will lay sinews upon you, and will cause flesh to come upon you, and cover you with skin, and put breath in you, and you shall live; and you shall know that I am the Lord'.
So I prophesied as I was commanded; and as I prophesied, there was a noise, and behold, a rattling; and the bones came together, bone to its bone. And as I looked, there were sinews on them, and flesh had come upon them, and skin had covered them; but there was no breath in them.
Then he said to me, 'Prophesy to the breath, prophesy, son of man, and say to the breath, Thus says the Lord God: Come from the four winds, O breath, and breathe upon these slain, that they may live'.
So I prophesied as he commanded me, and the breath came into them, and they lived, and stood upon their feet, an exceedingly great host.

It is the breath or spirit which gives life. The prophet is a minister of the Word of God who carries out an order. Even though we are dealing with a vision and not a liturgical action, we can extend its symbolic significance to other contexts, including the liturgical context which we are seeking to understand.

In a penitential prayer, the penitent invokes, 'Create in me again a steadfast spirit... and a willing spirit sustain in me' (Ps 51:12.14). In the form of a proclamation, a hymn to creation says, 'If you take away their breath they die and return to dust. You send forth your spirit and they are created, and you renew the face of the earth'. It would be enough to change the proclamation into an invocation to have an epiclesis.

3. *Epiclesis of consecration.* To begin, let us introduce the four invocations to the Spirit in the Eucharistic celebration. The first is in the Penitential Liturgy. The second is in the Liturgy of the Word. The third is for the consecration, and the fourth is for communion. The first two do not appear explicitly in ancient or modern texts. Experts tell us that the third and fourth are really one, expressed under two aspects. They indicate that they were once united and they complain that the present text has separated them. Since it is my intention to explain them individually, I will take the new texts as they are actually used. The unity between consecration and communion will appear on various occasions.

I have spoken of new texts, because in the only Canon used before the Council it is difficult enough to discover the epiclesis. Perhaps the controversy with the Eastern Churches had a negative influence. We can trace it in the words, 'Sanctify, O God, these offerings... and be pleased to accept them... as a spiritual sacrifice'. In the adjective 'spiritual' we can spot the presence and action of the Spirit. The supplication is an invocation to the Father. It is for him to receive the offering of our gifts and transform them. Others find it in the words which immediately follow the Sanctus:

> We come to you, Father, with praise and thanksgiving, through Jesus Christ your Son. Through him we ask you to accept and bless these gifts we offer you in sacrifice.

It is an invocation to the Father over our gifts. To our 'blessing' (*bereka*, gift) responds the blessing of the Father. It consists in the transformation of the gifts. But it is difficult to find in these words the theme of the Spirit.

In the new texts (which for the most part are more ancient) the epiclesis is clearly expressed. The second Canon – or anaphora, or prayer – is the most ancient and closely follows a text of Hippolytus. Already the preface or prologue has confessed that the Son of God, the Word, 'took flesh... by the power of the Holy Spirit'.

After the Sanctus comes the petition:

> Let your Spirit come upon these gifts to make them holy [Latin: *sanctifica*], so that they may become for us the body and blood of our Lord, Jesus Christ.

Such a petition addresses itself to the Father asking for the gift of the Spirit. 'Sanctifying' is the equivalent of consecrating, making holy or sacred. We ask that our gifts may cease to be ordinary bread and wine, and begin to be a holy reality, the body and blood of the glorified Lord. How can this mystery be accomplished? By the outpouring of the Holy Spirit. The term 'outpouring' or 'effusion' comes from the Old Testament. Although it makes little sense to us to speak of 'pouring out breath', in Hebrew there is an expression, *sapak ruh* (the verb can take as its object liquid, solid or gaseous substances):

Ez 39:29	I will pour out my Spirit upon the house of Israel.
Joel 3:1-2	And it shall come to pass afterward, that I will pour out my spirit on all flesh.
Zech 12:10	And I will pour out... a spirit of compassion.

Just as we speak of an outpouring or effusion, we could speak of an infusion. Even in the texts we cited from Joel or Zechariah, it is possible to read, 'I will pour in'. It is a way of approaching the mystery and mentally outlining it.

Moreover we must take note of the trinitarian concentration of the formula. We ask the Father to send the Spirit, in order to make the Son present. Sometimes one must reflect upon or explain such dense and rich expressions. The priest pronounces the epiclesis after the Sanctus (which did not exist in the most ancient Eucharistic Prayers). With the words of the Book of Isaiah, the whole community has proclaimed the holiness of God. Now, through the president of the liturgy, the community asks that this holiness concern itself and reveal itself in the sanctification which will happen when the Holy Spirit shall breathe or be poured into our gifts.

The third Anaphora puts all this in these terms:

> And so, Father, we bring you these gifts. We ask you to make them holy [Latin: *sanctificare*] by the power of your Spirit, so that they may become the body and blood of your Son, our Lord Jesus Christ.

Immediately beforehand it is proclaimed that the Father through the power of the Holy Spirit gives life and holiness to all creation. The life-giving action which Ezekiel evocatively described will continue in the sanctifying action. A climactic moment will be the 'sanctification' or consecration of the gifts. We have offered them, separating them from ordinary use, setting them apart and bringing them as a humble and sincere gift. To our *beraka* there responds the consecration on the part of the Spirit.

The fourth Anaphora is a modern composition, but it makes use of many ancient elements or is inspired by them. It is the most extensive and solemn, and we should listen to it too, beginning with the paragraphs which follow the Sanctus.

The action of the Spirit is proclaimed at two moments: one is the Incarnation, the other is Pentecost. In both cases the subject is the Son:

> He sent the holy Spirit from you, Father, as his first gift to those who believe, to complete his work on earth and bring us the fullness of grace.

The Spirit is the first-fruits, the first and greatest gift. It is a dynamic gift which has begun and should not delay in sanctifying and consecrating everything. Although this text does not say so explicitly, the consecration of all things will take place according to the condition and function of every creature. The centre is humanity, and within it is that 'summoned' group that is the Church.

Following this preparation, the Anaphora reaches the epiclesis, which is formulated thus:

> Father, may this holy Spirit sanctify these offerings. Let them become the body and blood of Jesus Christ Lord.

In conclusion, beyond all controversy, the Eucharist is an intense action of the Spirit in the

Church, perhaps the most intense. Polarized by the body of Christ among us, trained to a cordial (even polemical?) veneration of his permanent presence, we must not forget the action of the Spirit. We could say that nothing is more charismatic than the Eucharistic celebration. If the rhythm and movement of the liturgy does not leave space for reflection, if our attention tires and does not notice the moment of the epiclesis, we need extra moments and times to recover the Christian understanding of the matter.

4. *Epiclesis of communion.* I have already said that originally there were not two epicleses, but one in two parts, now separated by the consecration narrative.

We must start from a principle. The Body of Christ is the sanctified and consecrated gift. But no less Body of Christ is the Church, although in another way. To this we add another consideration. From the same Greek root come both the Greek word *epiclesis*, invocation, and the word *ekklesia*, convocation. The Church, convoked by the Word of the Gospel, now invokes the Spirit so that he may sanctify-consecrate the gifts and offerings, making them both the Body of Christ.

It is not that the change now happens radically for the first time. This human group that makes up a local Church is already the Body of Christ, and only because it is can it celebrate the Eucharist, which is not an individual devotion. When we begin by saying, 'The Lord be with you – and also with you', the Christian community already exists. It has already responded to the radical convocation, making it present in this assembly. In the Eucharist the Christian messianic community which expresses, consolidates and strengthens itself already exists, and does not begin now to be the Body of Christ. All the same, the Body can grow in stature, in cohesiveness and in vitality, as Jesus of Nazareth 'grew up and became strong, full of wisdom, and the favour of God was upon him' (Lk 2:40). 'And Jesus grew in wisdom, age and grace before God and men' (Lk 2:52).

The Christian community, which is already the Body of Christ, must 'take body', becoming ever more the Body of Christ 'until we arrive at maturity, to that development which pertains to the full maturity of Christ' (Eph 4:13). Christ will be present bodily, alive in the consecrated gifts, in order that he may be bodily whole in his community. It is as if there has been a peaceful encounter man to man[1] in the embrace of gifts and community; body and Body of Christ.

How will the transformation be achieved? Who is the agent? When Samuel prepares to anoint king Saul, he explains to him secretly what is going to happen:

1 Sam 10:1 Then Samuel took a vial of oil and poured it on his head, and kissed him and said,

2 'Has not the Lord anointed you to be prince over his people Israel?...

6 Then the spirit of the Lord will come mightily upon you... and you shall be turned into another man.

7 Now when these signs meet you, do whatever your hand finds to do, for God is with you'.

In the book of Judges are described some of Samson's violent exploits:

---

[1] Translator's note: In Spanish, *'entablar un cuerpo a cuerpo pacífico'*.

Judg 14:6 The Spirit of the Lord came mightily upon him, and he tore the lion asunder as one tears a kid.

19 And the Spirit of the Lord came mightily upon him, and he went down to Ashkelon and killed thirty men of the town, and took their spoil and gave the festal garments to those who had told the riddle.

15:14 The Spirit of the Lord came mightily upon him, and the ropes which were on his arms became as flax that has caught fire, and his bonds melted off his hands.

Saul is the legitimate leader of the community, Samson a sniper against the invading Philistines. What interests us in these examples is the invasion by the Spirit which transforms the man. The same Spirit can transform a community:

Eph 4:3 Be eager to maintain the unity of the Spirit in the bond of peace. There is one body and one Spirit....

5. *Liturgical formulae.* The second Anaphora or Canon says this:

> May all of us who share in the body and blood of Christ be brought together in unity by the Holy Spirit.

'To congregate' comes from the word *grex* = a flock, which the shepherd keeps united and protects it from being scattered. Without using the word 'body', the text mentions 'unity', because a body is an organic unity, not an agglomeration or a juxtaposition. The Eucharist presupposes the union of members. It would be a contradiction to celebrate it when the unity is compromised. With the Eucharist, the existing unity is expressed and strengthened.

In an earlier chapter I spoke of the new circulation of blood in the Body of Christ which is the

Church. The blood which circulates brings oxygen to every member, to every tissue, to every cell. The Eucharistic blood brings the Spirit to all the members of the community, giving it vitality and tightening its unity.

The third Anaphora or prayer fairly quickly opens doors and windows to the penetration of the Spirit. Prolonging the Sanctus, as we have seen, it proclaims:

> Father, you are holy indeed, and all creation rightly gives you praise. All life, all holiness comes from you through your Son, Jesus Christ our Lord, by the working [Latin: *operante virtute*] of the Holy Spirit. From age to age you gather [Latin: *congregare non desinis*] a people to yourself...

It proclaims the dynamism, the 'power' of the Spirit, as source of life and universal consecration, as the centre which gathers the community together again. Impelled by this wind which forces us along without scattering us, we listen to the epiclesis:

> Look with favour on your Church's offering, and see the Victim whose death has reconciled us to yourself. Grant that we, who are nourished by his body and blood, may be filled with his Holy Spirit, and become one body, one spirit in Christ.

The community is going to receive nourishment, food and drink, which will strengthen it as an organism. Through the body and blood of Christ the community is filled again with the Spirit which the glorified Christ always communicates to his Church. In this way the community forms with Christ its head one body and one spirit. The purpose of communion is to nourish the community, not to sanctify the individual. The unity, which is expressed in the external assembly, is truly born from within, by a breath or Spirit which keeps it close together and alive. The epiclesis invokes the Spirit so that he might transform a group of people into a Christian community, the Body of Christ.

The fourth Anaphora confirms all we are saying:

> By your Holy Spirit, gather all who share this one bread and one cup into the one body of Christ, a living sacrifice of praise [Latin: *ut, in unum corpus a Sancto Spirito congregati, in Christo hostia viva perficiantur, ad laudem gloriae tuae*].

One is the bread, and one is the cup, while many are those who share it. Sharing is already an act of unity. The invasion of the Spirit comes about and the unity is effectively made present from within.

We have reviewed three variations of the epiclesis for the consecration and as many for the communion. An important conclusion is the primary function of the Spirit in the Church's becoming the Body of Christ. There will be suitable and necessary external instruments of organization so that our Church may be a social body. But let us not forget that the action of the Spirit is primary and decisive. If this were missing, it would be useless to make plans, organize, issue laws and directives, and have everything foreseen and controlled. We would have a model enterprise, an exemplary society, but a community of men and women is the Body of Christ when it is sustained and animated by the Spirit of Christ, and this is the sense of the eucharistic epiclesis.

6. *Epiclesis of penance?* I have already noted that the penitential formula of absolution (which I do not call sacramental) takes the form of an invocation to the Father or almighty God. The priest does not say,

'I forgive you your sins' but asks that God may 'have mercy on us, forgive us our sins, and bring us to everlasting life'. He asks in the name of the ecclesial community, including himself among those who need pardon. But there is no mention of the Spirit.

Two biblical texts will help us fill this gap. The first is taken from the most famous penitential prayer in the Old Testament, Psalm 51. After a repeated confession of sins, wrong-doings, faults and perversity, the penitent asks for a new creation by God: 'Create in me, O God...'. In this prayer the Spirit will be present:

Ps 51:10 Put a new and steadfast spirit within me.
11 Take not thy holy Spirit from me.
12 Uphold me with a willing spirit.

It is the most beautiful penitential prayer to the Spirit in the whole Bible (I have commented on it in my book, *Treinta Salmos. Poesía y oración,* pp. 217ff). A spirit which may give consistency from within, which may oppose the 'broken bones'; a steadfast spirit which replaces the 'contrite' (= broken) spirit; a 'holy' spirit which relieves it and consecrates it, replacing and making up for the ritual 'sacrifices'; a generous spirit, which can be the new dynamic principle of life and action – not externally, but internally, not a law, but a generous spontaneity.

This petition has a significant resonance in the prophecy of Ezekiel:

36:25 I will sprinkle clean water upon you, and you shall be clean from all your uncleannesses, and from all your idols I will cleanse you.
26 A new heart I will give you, and a new spirit I will put within you; and I will take out of your flesh the heart of stone and give you a heart of flesh.

27 And I will put my spirit within you, and cause you to walk in my statutes and be careful to observe my ordinances.

28 You shall dwell in the land which I gave to your fathers; and you shall be my people, and I will be your God.

Our second text may be taken from the Gospel of John. The link between the Spirit and forgiveness is explicit:

Jn 20:22 And when he had said this, he breathed on them, and said to them, 'Receive the Holy Spirit;

23 If you forgive the sins of any, they are forgiven; if you retain the sins of any, they are retained'.

There is no sacrament if there is no forgiveness. There is no forgiveness without the action of the Spirit.

7. *Epiclesis of the word?* This too is not explicit in the liturgical texts. One can probably see a 'relic' of an epiclesis in the words with which the president blesses the reader, 'May the Lord be on your heart and on your lips that you may worthily proclaim the Gospel'. We may think that the presence in the heart and on the lips may be the presence of the Spirit.

The reason is clear and simple. We call the Bible the 'inspired word'. The adjective signifies that the word is formed and uttered by being inspired and fashioned by the Spirit. Under the touch and impulse of this divine breath, a human experience is transformed into a word of communication. This makes it an inspired word. The linguistic structure which is a text is preserved in a conventional piece of writing or book – the Scripture, writ. But the writing is not the word, as the score is not the music.

The writing preserves the text, and the linguistic structure contains potentially the breath which it has aroused. The word must come to presence in the reader and listeners so that it really returns to existence. But it must spring forth inspired by the same breath, and must be received by those in tune with it.

The Council Constitution *Dei Verbum* tells us that Scripture 'must be read and interpreted with the same Spirit with which it was written' or composed (DV 12). The Liturgy surrounds the reading with a certain ceremonial to indicate that we are not dealing with just any reading. At the end, the assembly confirms everything proclaimed as 'the word of God, the word of the Lord'. It would be possible to insert an epiclesis at the beginning. One can do it especially in some liturgies or paraliturgies of the Word.

At least we are aware of the reality. In the inspired word it is the Spirit made word which is communicated. In the shared hearing of one text the Spirit invades us, penetrates us and unifies us.

I conclude this reflection on the epiclesis by repeating what I have already said: there is nothing more charismatic than the celebration of the Eucharist.

8. ANAMNESIS – MEMORY

Anamnesis is a Greek word (as is *epiclesis*) which means remembrance. From the same root we derive our words amnesia, mnemonics. It is applied traditionally to that part of the Eucharist which consists in the recalling to the memory, remembering. In a technical sense we could distinguish and oppose anamnesis and epiclesis, as a text in which we narrate and a text in which we invoke. Regarding the controversy about this, the two books I quoted at the beginning by Gesteira and Sanchez Caro, give information at a different level. My intention is not so much historical or systematic, as explanatory. I would like us to penetrate by reflection to the meaning and the implications of our Eucharist as memory.

1. Memory – something so simple, so obvious, so marvellous; so obvious that we do not see it, so well known that we do not reflect upon it. We speak of 'sense-memory' in which even animals participate. Here I am referring to the conscious memory, as an act of the human spirit. The memory is correlative to our being in time. It allows us to make present facts and data which are far away in space and time. What a capacity for content has an average memory! How it stretches like elastic to increase its capacity! If we took a person of average education and began to count and arrange all the data stored in their memory, we would be surprised. When someone says to me 'How many things you know!', I reply,

'And you too, only you know other things'. In what way is a computer better than us? In the sheer amount of data, perhaps. What about connections? What about the integration of data into coherent unity? What about the aliveness = 'life' with which data return from infancy, what about emotional vibrations? We are not speaking of a mechanism but of consciousness.

In what recesses, in what storerooms is this innumerable data kept? How are they maintained, dormant yet vigilant, in order to present themselves when necessary? What mechanism makes them spring to mind, whether they are invoked or not? We say: Now I remember, I don't remember, I have it on the tip of my tongue, I try to remember, I want to refresh my memory... Where does the 'thing' come from which 'refreshes' the memory, how does consciousness become separated from 'the tip of the tongue'?

The Hebrews had an elementary anthropology, more tied to corporeity. What one experiences with the feelings, what one hears, penetrates into the heart, and from here descends into certain inner parts of the body where they are stored:

Prov 18:8	The words of a whisperer are like delicious morsels; they go down into the inner parts of the body. They remain hidden, accessible only to God and the mind.
Prov 20:27	The spirit of man is the lamp of the Lord, searching all his innermost parts.

From those depths 'they rise up to the heart' and become conscious cf. Is 65:17; Jer 3:16; 7:31; etc.

Today, we have available a more sophisticated knowledge which is less material. But do we really succeed in explaining the activity of the memory? Or does it continue to be largely a mystery, one of so many mysteries which we are and which we harbour? The memory also exercises other important functions. It is the condition for our psychological identity. An attack of amnesia can reach the point where a patient 'has broken (not breaks) with the past', he no longer knows who he is. Thanks to the memory, our mind preserves its personal identity through time and its changes.

We can think of a memory that is simply cognitive; like a show which we put on within ourselves, which we attend with enjoyment, serene and detached. Usually, the memory is more than a self-sufficient spectacle, and it becomes a dynamic factor. The past has modelled us, action by action. In a moment, a fact from our past appears, charged with challenge, ready to model our next action. Repentance cannot cancel out the deed, but it can prevent its consequences. It can transform the error or fault into an impulse for good. We learn at our own expense. Other moments return, showering illusion, courage. The memory does not resuscitate the past event but loads and launches its potential:

Deut 7:18 You shall not be afraid of them, but you shall remember what the Lord your God did to Pharaoh and to all Egypt...

9:6 For you are a stubborn people: remember how you provoked the Lord.

15:15 You shall not let your slave go empty-handed...You shall remember that you were a slave in the land of Egypt.

24:17 You shall not pervert the justice due to the sojourner or to the fatherless, or take a widow's garment in pledge; but you shall remember that you were a slave in Egypt and the Lord your God redeemed you from there.

2. *Social Memory.* What I have said about the individual is true in its way of the community. There exists a communitarian memory of the past, a shared memory. A group of people who do not share any memories do not form a society. Even very small societies, the family or clan, possess or cultivate their common memories. 'Family memories', they call them, stories or legends of the clan or tribe. If we extend our scope to a people or nation we would speak of chronicles or of history. The undertaking of Alfonso the Wise in composing the General Chronicle and the General History, was not a purely intellectual exercise. The need is so great that sometimes peoples invented a history, drawing from the mine of legend (Romulus and Remus or parts of our ancient novels). The force is so great that the immigrant or his children end up appropriating the history of others which strictly speaking does not belong to them. Often societies have professionals charged with preserving and bringing alive the collective memory. Those who record it are epic singers or historiographers, those who recite it may be bards or professors. Deep within them they have rooms in which they keep recordings of facts which they hold for the appropriate time: they are the archives.

The memory of special events is brought to life in the form of a festive celebration: Independence Day, Victory Day, the day of a discovery, of a voyage round the world or the day on which someone stood on the moon for the first time (when the phrase 'estar en la luna' = 'to stand on the moon' changed its meaning). The community must take part in the celebration so that it can be public and collective. There can also be sad memories but these are an exception.

Israel as a society used its memory with particular intensity because in its glorious deeds a protagonist is proclaimed who is the Lord. The memory of Israel is the history of the people, which could not have happened without the intervention of God and would be incomprehensible without confessing him. Israel not only uses its memory but has a law about it, as Psalm 78 indicates:

> 3 ...things that we have heard and known,
> that our fathers have told us.
> 4 We will not hide them from their children,
> but tell to the coming generation
> the glorious deeds of the Lord, and his might,
> and the wonders which he has wrought.
> 5 He established a testimony in Jacob,
> and appointed a law in Israel,
> 6 which he commanded our fathers
> to teach to their children;
> that the next generation might know them,
> the children yet unborn,
> 7 and arise and tell them to their children,
> so that they should set their hope in God,
> and not forget the works of God...

A large part of the Old Testament sprang up not only from the observations and fantasies of its writers but above all from the urgent need to tell the story. To remember is a grateful duty, to forget is a crime.

Moreover, Israel established celebrations and feasts to commemorate major events or to give historical content to already existing agricultural festivals. The Passover must recall the Exodus from Egypt; the Feast of Tabernacles, the crossing of the desert. There were also penitential celebrations. It is amazing that in these the Hebrews felt themselves to be in solidarity with their ancestors and with one another. The sorrowful confession of sin unites them:

Ps 106:6	Both we and our fathers have sinned; we have committed iniquity, we have done wickedly.
Bar 1:19	From the day when the Lord brought our fathers out of the land of Egypt until today, we have been disobedient to the Lord our God, and we have been negligent, in not heeding his voice.

Celebration for Israel was to return to a common matrix, as if to hear the murmur of common roots buried in a common land.

The Israelites remembered the legends and stories of the patriarchs. They remembered especially the foundational event, the liberation from Egypt. Invoking the name of the Lord, they added the title, 'He who led us out of Egypt'. Their profession of faith is a profession of deeds, not of doctrine. Many times the Psalms stop to recall the facts of history. Sometimes the individual remembers his past experience of God. Wisdom literature, which in the beginning flowed at the edge of history, at a certain point opened its doors to it.

3. *Christian memory.* From this background of humanity in general and Israel in particular, we can come to our topic, and find it illuminated and even explained. The Christian people inherited the habit and urgency of remembering. The Eucharist is a festive, communitarian memory. Besides, thanksgiving *(beraka)* is memory. Perhaps these are two sides of the same coin. To persons who have done us a big favour we are grateful, and we show it with words and acts of regard (= *beraka*): we recall with gratitude their birthday or the day they saved

our life by sending them a greetings card and a present. The Eucharist is a pleasing remembrance, linked with esteem for the one who saved our life. It festively recalls the foundational event of our salvation. As a festive memory it has a fixed content, a variable content and a multiple purpose.

The fixed content is the event which concentrates all the others, the death and resurrection of the Lord, the sacrifice through which he frees us and through which he passed from death to life. There is no substitute for this nucleus; this event, which is both fundamental and climactic, cannot be forgotten. We have a command from the Lord, 'Do this in memory of me'. All the Eucharistic Prayers or anaphorae agree on this point. This time I will quote from the first Anaphora, the Roman Canon:

> Father, we celebrate the memory of Christ, your Son. We, your people and your ministers, recall [Latin: *'Unde et memores, Domine, nos servi tui, sed et plebs tua sancta, eiusdem Christi, Filii tui, Domini nostri*] his passion, his resurrection from the dead, and his ascension into glory; and from the many gifts you have given us we offer to you, God of glory and majesty....

(Even in the debated anaphora of Addai and Mari, in which the words of the Last Supper are not quoted, there does appear the explicit reference 'celebrating this mystery... of the passion, death and resurrection of our Lord Jesus Christ'. See the cited book of Sanchez Caro, pp.108-138).

The moment of the death and resurrection presupposes and includes a series of events, a whole life, from conception to birth, continuing with the growth, teaching, miracles and other deeds. Even these can be the object of 'variable', occasional memory. The Eucharist will always remember the death and resurrection. On one day it will also remember the birth, on another the arrival of the Magi, another the Baptism, another the Transfiguration. On the one hand this practice breaks the monotony, on the other it centres all the deeds around the capital event. The liturgical 'cycle' or circumference thus has its centre.

The variety can be appreciated above all in the prefaces, in such a way that the life of the Church, the fruit and result of salvation, also enters the memory. The Liturgical reform has given more space to the introduction of special prefaces.

After having considered the fixed and variable contents, we must reflect on the purpose of the Eucharistic memory. Given what we have said above, it will be easy to understand the purpose of thanking God for his benefits. We can see the purpose of memory as a guarantee of *identity*. Our *Christian* identity comes from Christ. The adjective next to the noun seems to be a tautology, but it is necessary to repeat it. Our Christian identity is rooted in the death and resurrection of our Saviour. For this reason we must remember it. The explicit remembering identifies us both internally and externally as a community. This is our identity document. The Church will not suffer from a collective attack of amnesia and forget where it comes from, though some members can suffer one. So, is the Eucharist simply a 'Sunday Obligation', in which the formality of satisfying it is more important than its content? The Sunday or Dominical Obligation means the obligation of the Lord (= *Domini*), and he commands, 'Do this', because, by remembering, we are.

So, we pass to the other function, that of memory

as a *principle of action.* The remembering of sins belonged to the penitential liturgy. Now we remember the benefits which urge us to thanksgiving. Moreover, they are exemplary benefits, which impel us to an imitation of them. If our identity is rooted in and germinates from a sacrifice out of love, we cannot continue in egoism as a way of life. Every moment of the life of Christ speaks to us, challenges us and demands of us a 'con-form-ity', that is a shared 'common form'. If the contrary were true, the memory would be a mockery. The memory is the principle and guarantee of our identity; the energetic, active memory is the principle of identification. We are of Christ, and we must be ever more like Christ. His memory urges us on, and this not only as individuals, but as a community.

1 Pet 2:21 Christ suffered for you, leaving you an example, that you should follow in his steps.

4. *Remembering and hope.* As well as the enormous service it does us, the memory can also set a trap for us. This happens when it changes into nostalgia for an unrecoverable past. We take no delight in the present, pay no more attention to the future, we close ourselves in a mental refuge which is constructed from the remnants of the past. It is all an exhibition of pictures representing happy and glorious moments which did in part exist but which are partly figments of the imagination. There we take refuge with ever greater frequency in order to reject the present and the future. From there we hurl condemnations against the present times, which we do not consider our own; 'in my day...'.

Some exiles in Babylon cultivated a nostalgia which paralyzed them and blinded them. Deutero-

Isaiah, the prophet of the exile and return, seemed to abolish the law of memory when he said:

Is 43:18-19 Remember not the former things, nor consider the things of old. Behold I am doing a new thing; now it springs forth, do you not perceive it?.

They looked so much to the past that they did not see the future sprouting up. It was as if God had nothing left to do, and the people had nothing to hope for, as if all their encounters with God were concentrated in the past, and there was nothing left to live for.

So, there also exists a memory of the future. To hope is to remember. It is to make the future present, sometimes in the knowledge of what will be, at other times without guessing it. 'A little thing will be your first condition, compared with the greatness which the future holds' (Job 8:7).

If you do not like the word 'remember', we can replace it with 'to hold present'. The Hebrew verb ***zkr*** means precisely 'to hold present':

Is 47:7 ...you did not lay these things to heart or remember (*zkr*) their end.
Lam 1:9 ...she took no thought (*zkr*) of her doom.
Sir 38:20 Do not give your heart to sorrow; drive it away, remembering the end of life.
41:3 Remember your former days and the end of life.

Or, with a different nuance, one remembers an announcement or promise of the past whose content belongs to the future.

This is decisive for the Christian life. We do not live only from the past, we live as much for the future. The Lord, who has come, must come again. Our encounter with God is not only in the past, it is also in the present and the future. The whole history of the Church is like a great journey, taut and intense, between Christ who has come and Christ who will come. He is the journey. When we finish our reading of the Bible, the last words are, 'Come, Lord Jesus'. Even while the book is closed, it remains definitively open.

Our renewed liturgy knows how to express and inculcate it with new emphases. The first Anaphora (the Roman Canon), which I quoted above, ended with the Ascension. Not so the new or renewed ones. If our memories are glorious, our hope is joyful. For this reason the assembly can celebrate a joyful memory.

Let us linger over the acclamations after the consecration. The priest says, 'Let us proclaim the mystery of faith', that is, this is the sacrament, the summary and sign of our faith, which is our adhesion, our engagement with the Lord. The people reply, in the third formula, 'Christ has died, Christ is risen, Christ will come again'. (In Latin: *Mortem tuam annuntiamus, Domine, et tuam resurrectionem confitemur, donec venias.*) Rooted in the past, we open ourselves to the future. The present festival embraces everything. In the third formula the acclamation rings out, 'When we eat this bread and drink this cup, we proclaim your death, Lord Jesus, until you come in glory'. (In Latin: *Quotiescumque manducamus panem hunc et calicem bibimus, mortem tuam annuntiabimus, Domine, donec venias.*) The Resurrection is implicit. If the Lord will return, it means he is alive, and until that moment our acclamation will resound full of hope, the hope of the individual and of the Church. The fourth formula simply says, 'Lord, by your cross and resurrection you have set us free. You are the Saviour of the world.' [In Latin: *Salvator mundi, salva nos, qui per crucem et resurrectionem tuam liberasti nos.*]

After the acclamations, common to all the anaphorae, the memory is different in some versions. The third Anaphora, after the remembrance of the Ascension, adds, 'ready to greet him when he comes again'. The fourth Anaphora says the same. The theme resounds in other passages too:

> let us be filled with grace and blessing [*omni benedictione et gratia repleamur*] (Anaphora I);
> make us worthy to share eternal life [*aeternae vitae mereamur esse consortes*] (Anaphora II);
> may he... enable us to share in the inheritance of your saints [*cum electis tuis haereditatem consequi valeamus*] (Anaphora III);
> grant also to us, your children, to enter into our heavenly inheritance [*nobis omnibus, filiis tuis, clemens Pater, concede, ut caelestem hereditatem consequi valeamus*] (Anaphora IV).

So the present dimension of our Eucharistic celebration is enclosed between the memory of the first coming of Christ and the memory-hope of the final coming.

I cannot make the final point. Because the Eucharistic memory is not pure remembering, but in it reality comes about. The Lord, died and risen, makes himself present sacramentally, and future life is in fact communicated. It is not only a remembering, but that does not take away from the fact that it is memory, anamnesis.

9. CONSECRATION – TRANSFORMATION

As in the preceding reflections, it is not my intention to offer a scientific or systematic study of the theme, nor to give a learned popularization of what has already been studied by others. I content myself with illuminating some important aspects of our Eucharist, with reflections from the Old Testament and meditations on these.

1. *The consecration.* Some will certainly remember the time when they were children or young, when the consecration was presented as the central moment, the climax, of the eucharistic celebration. It was surrounded with a display of mystery and particular solemnity. Either it took place in total silence, or the 'royal march' was played, as the homage of the people to their Lord who was present. Even the most important people knelt down or genuflected at that moment. After each of the two consecrations the priest elevated the host and chalice with arms held high, so that the people could see and adore. Various genuflections articulated the action.

This practice had a catechetical purpose. It imposed a sense of mystery, instilled reverence and humility, and provoked an intense act of faith. But along with these valuable things, there could also creep in some notable distortions. The moment remained disconnected from the unified dynamic of the celebration. Its intensity dampened what went before and what came afterwards. Communion had little importance, and the preceding parts almost slipped away. Of these distortions I believe that the most notable was the loss of the sense of unity of the celebration. I think that today it is easier to overcome this difficulty, partly because the texts are pronounced in the language of the people and partly because the new, or ancient, anaphorae develop a simpler, linear scheme.

Because of this profound unity, I wanted to anticipate some of the elements when I explained the 'offertory = *beraka*' formula. The current reflection makes sense in continuity with this.

2. *Transformation.* In our upbringing the term 'consecration' was associated exclusively with the words taken from a narrative text, that is, a couple of sentences from the account of the Last Supper, spoken by Jesus over the bread and the cup. The narrative introduction and the institutional command 'Do this in memory of me', remained outside, even though they were adjacent. The Eastern Churches would refer the effect to the epiclesis, and many contemporary theologians would insist on considering the liturgical action as a unity.

All of them have analyzed and explained this aspect of the Eucharist in terms of real transformation (not a purely mental act). The particle 'trans' means change or mutation: transfiguration, transition, transubstantiation, transfinalization. Starting from a stable situation, there comes a moment of transition, which leads into a new stable situation. The stability can be relative. We pause for now at the moment of transition, which can be a process, or an instant.

What is a moment, or an instant, in our empirical perception?

Stability and change are the two categories of which I avail myself in order to confront a mystery without pretending to exhaust it. Analogy and symbol will be my instrument to go around in a spiral which approaches but never arrives. I need a broad base on which to situate our action, a base of experience and culture which may lift and sustain our reflection. To lift ourselves high, the base must be wide.

3. *Steadiness and change.* There are persons, epochs and cultures which give greater importance to stability, while others are more sensitive to change. Whereas one people or epoch may live better in stability, others live and experience evolution and even revolution.

What is the Biblical mentality in the Old Testament?

It presupposes and values stability, without closing its eyes to change.

The first chapter of Genesis is a late text which uses for its poetic and theological vision a fixed cultural scheme. God creates by distinguishing and fixing beings, natures and functions. Sun, moon, stars; upper and lower waters, and a vault to separate them; seas and continents; and living beings, each 'according to their own species'. All is fixed from the beginning, and must not be disordered. A man must not plough with the ox and the ass, one must not weave wool and linen, one sex must not wear the clothes of the other, because this would be to mix and confound, going against the order of creation (according to one school of thought and behaviour). Distinction and stability remain sealed in a system of names given by God himself: 'He called it day, night, sea'. Even human beings appear already distinguished as male and female.

If changes happen, it is like a breach of the established order, and there can be a catastrophe. Catastrophe is a Greek word which denotes an inversion, a revolution (*kata-strepho*). A good example would be the flood which mixes the waters above and the waters below, and confounds continents with oceans. Such was the destruction of Sodom and Gomorrah, which upset prosperous cities and fertile country with fire. The earthquake is a pathological and numinous shaking of the stable earth (as if it had become like the ocean). Stability is the theme and preoccupation of the writers. Above all there is exalted and asserted the sovereignty of God, which can instigate a change, whether catastrophic or beneficial (Is 45:18; Jer 10:12; Ps 24:2; 104:5):

Is 45:18	(God) formed the earth and made it, he established it.
Jer 10:12	He established the world by his wisdom.
Ps 24:2	He founded the world upon the seas, and established it upon the rivers.
Ps 104:5	Thou didst set the earth on its foundations, so that it should never be shaken.

In his great imprecation, Job asks that an eclipse may obscure the earth, that the darkness may take possession of the light (ch. 3); it is a return to primordial chaos.

Simplifying the data, we have arrived at the binomial of stability and catastrophe. Against this background we are surprised by the last chapter of the Old Testament – last, that is, in chronology, not in the present arrangement of the biblical books. The book is probably contemporaneous with Christ. It is of Greek origin, and belongs to the Wisdom corpus. It is called the Book of Wisdom. Because of its nature and the time it was written it can contemplate history in its totality and propose a synthesis of it. Because of its frontier position, it mixes Greek influences with the tradition of Israel. I will quote entirely the finale of the book:

Wis 19:18 For the elements changed places with one another,
as on a harp the notes vary the nature of the rhythm,
while each note remains the same.
This may be clearly inferred from the sight of what took place.

19 For land animals were transformed into water creatures,
and creatures that swim moved over to the land.

20 Fire even in water retained its normal power,
and water forgot its fire-quenching nature.

21 Flames, on the contrary, failed to consume
the flesh of perishable creatures that walked among them,
nor did they melt the crystalline, easily melted kind of heavenly food.

22 For in everything, O Lord, thou has exalted and glorified thy people;
and thou hast not neglected to help them at all times and in all places.

Here enters the theory of the elements and their marvellous transmutation, all happening through divine power for the sake of salvation. The crossing of the Red Sea is the raising up of dry land where the sea used to extend. The manna does not dissolve under the rays of the sun.

The musical comparison of the author is interesting too. I do not think he is an expert in music, but he seems to have had some of the ideas that were current in his day, perhaps of Pythagorean origin. The important thing is the system of correspondences (I quote from my commentary in *Los Libros sagrados*):

> unity of the instrument / unity of the universe; permanence of sounds / permanence of the elements, variation of melodies or tones / variations in the function of the elements, with a harmonious result on both levels. Music, by analogy, makes comprehensible a mystery of the divine action; as a musician and composer, God knows how to create unity from multiplicity. He establishes laws and proportions, and changes them without destroying their harmony. Instead of the 'music of the spheres' we are dealing with the harmony of the cosmos and of history as variations on a theme of salvation.

This late writer takes up suggestions already put forward by others, e.g., Deutero-Isaiah or some Psalms:

> 107:33 He turns rivers into a desert,
> springs of water into thirsty ground...
> 35 He turns a desert into pools of water,
> a parched land into springs of water.

Rather than expound a biblical theme, I have proposed a scheme constructed on a couple of citations: stability, catastrophe, transformation. It is one component of the base which I was proposing to set up before continuing.

4. I take the other component from our modern culture, dynamism and transformation. In our present culture, we appreciate a preference for change, dynamism, and evolution over stability. We do not oppose stability; without counting on a certain sta-

bility, no science would be possible. But it is a stability of processes. Laws known and formulated, even though they are based on statistics, allow us to operate.The universe we contemplate today is a *perpetuum mobile.*

We can begin with the inorganic, from those stars which up to a few centuries ago were thought to be made up of incorruptible matter and to be perfectly stable in their untiring movement. All this is gone. The sun is for us a mass which is being consumed in a process of fusion and fission, spreading energy around which puts into motion infinite processes on earth. And we are not talking simply of stars. We distinguish white stars and red stars, novae and supernovae, nebulae and galaxies, all in continuous movement and transformation. And an energy called light which journeys and presents to our perception what happened millions of years ago...

Let us pass on to the little things: from the atom we have descended to particles, to watch slow or dizzy processes of mutation. What at first sight appears to be stable, is so because it has a time and rhythm different to ours. If we could change our rhythm, the ebb and flow of the sea would be a tic-tac, night and day a pulse-beat; then there would be the seasons; we would evaluate the disintegration of radio-active bodies as we see the wax melting close to the fire. We live immersed in a vortex of forces, limited by our time and our particular rhythms. When science succeeds in breaking and overcoming them, we stand looking in amazement at metamorphoses more fantastic than our fantasy. We pass on to vegetable life, which takes possession of the mineral to bring it to a new stage which is, in its turn, a continuous process. Can one reduce a cedar to a sum of physico-chemical processes? In what sense is the cedar identical to the seed from which it comes? Then animal life takes over the vegetable to raise it to the level of sensation in a qualitative leap. Even more radical is the qualitative leap from the mineral, vegetable and animal to the sphere of consciousness and freedom. Consciousness sustained by memory is the principle of the identity we possess, while the matter of our body renews itself at different rates. Even the life of consciousness is a process of lines, waves and leaps.

The human being contributes to the transmutation; observing and experimenting he interferes, begins processes and transforms. The same capacity to operate develops in a growing process, with notable qualitative leaps.

Let us now move on to language. According to Genesis 1, God establishes the name of the beings. According to Genesis 2, Adam fixes the species of animals in a system of appropriate names. Language as stability, even if the passing from being to experience to language is already a transformation. However, fantasy takes over; it starts to play with words and phrases, introducing that leap and comparison that is the metaphor: '*meta-phora* = trans-lation'. I return to the Book of Wisdom which I have already quoted, because this journey has a destination. I refer to the musical comparison. Nature is populated by sounds, cries and noises. The human being filters, stylizes and organizes them into systems we call scales, tones and modes. We think to ourselves, twelve temperate sounds, replayed in order of frequency. And from this handful of sounds is born an enchanted and mysterious host of songs, dances, suites, sonatas, symphonies and concertos.

The human being is the image of God too in its capacity to change, combine and produce new forms, without limit... He exults in so doing, he exults in what he has done. It is the human world of art.

5. *A different transformation*. We need all that has gone before in order to deal with a different kind of transformation. We must be well trained and accustomed to change in order to contemplate that new thing which is the mystery. It goes beyond all that has gone before, it draws it together and elevates it. It is the breaking in of God to the human sphere, it is God becoming man, it is a human nature assumed by a divine person. Never has a greater and more mysterious change than this happened in human history. It would justify all the stability and all the changes of the universe.

So, trained with the discipline of change, accustomed to the surprise of the leap, educated to imagine and expect more, we glimpse a change which overpowers us and we accept it joyfully and humbly – the incarnation.

The Son of God made man assumes the mineral, vegetable, animal and human world. His human nature is the 'microcosm', the unity of all creation, and, at the same time, the union of creation with God, in a mysterious way. It is the greatest change. We may believe in it without really understanding it, but our belief fills us with amazement and joy. There is a moment when his human figure lets another figure become transparent; he is transfigured. The three witnesses remain ecstatic, wishing to stay and contemplate him for ever. The Transfiguration is like a trans-parency of symbols. There is an impression of whitest light, very intense, without a shadow of darkness, as if the familiar body had turned itself into light (as if its matter had been transformed into energy). It was a momentary anticipation of the future change. The humanity assumed by the Son of God shares fully in the human experience, with the exception of sin, until death, death on the cross. But he passes through this death to glorification, which is the definitive change.

We must dwell on this point, because we cannot understand and ought not think of the eucharistic transformation except in terms of glorification. The imagination which helps us can deceive us. Artists represent Christ glorified with a bodiliness similar to what was there before, but radiant. We recall Michelangelo's athletic risen Christ with the cross. This was prompted by the Gospel accounts of the Resurrection, which present a body similar to the one before, as a guarantee of sensible identification, but endow it with superior qualities. Our imagination cannot portray things in any different way. But our mind can conceive them in another way. It can critically examine the images, or make use of them with an awareness of their limits.

Now, if we must use our imagination, let us seek help from modern science, which speaks to us of matter and energy, and of the transformation of matter into energy. Light is energy and is corporeal, whether we adopt the wave hypothesis or the corpuscular hypothesis.

Energy is not matter, but nor is it immaterial or spiritual. Let us imagine that the bodily form of the glorified one is formed of pure energy without matter. It will have new relations and qualities in space and time, intense concentration, diffused presence, unhampered mobility, action and communication...

A universe formed of pure energy would be corporeal and new. A glorified body composed of pure energy is an image, agreed, but is closer to the reality than in Michelangelo's statue of the Risen One or in the light and graceful figure of Fra Angelico.

6. Let us continue to imagine and reflect. With the Resurrection Christ has reached that definitive phase of transformation which the Transfiguration prefigured. It is an appointment for human beings, and for other creatures in a subordinate way. Through the energy of the Risen One, a piece of bread and a chalice of wine are drawn to and brought to this final and definitive moment for the salvation of humankind 'by the power which enables him even to subject all things to himself' (Phil 3:21). The energy of the Crucified One is concentrated in this circle of bread and volume of wine in order to communicate himself to humanity through them. We have already explained that this energy is his bodiliness. As the Transfiguration was an anticipation, so is the eucharistic transformation. At that time 'the figure' changed, offering to contemplation the intimate reality, though yet under the veil of appearances. Now, without a change of appearances his glorified body is offered at communion = communication. There is transmitted, in anticipation, a life that will be that definitive life.

I am imagining the manner of a real event. I am not describing a purely mental activity on the part of a believer. The Risen One really acts upon the bread and wine through the power of the Holy Spirit. He truly communicates his definitive life by means of these transformed elements.

I have employed images as an instrument of understanding and explanation. We are aware of their approximate and analogical character. What is important is that our point of departure is the glorification of Christ. It is not Christ in his mortal condition who is made present at the Eucharist, but it is the person of Christ who communicates himself by transfusing his life. His is a living body, the body of a Person.

The Eucharist is like a second bodily coming of the glorified Christ. It is an anticipated coming, as I explained in the chapter on memory. Observing it from the opposite point of view, I would say that it is a leap towards the definitive future of the gifts and of the community. Linking the two perspectives, I would say that it is a meeting of Christ with creation and with men and women, with creation represented by the bread and the wine (as we saw in the chapter on the offertory = *beraka*), with men and women represented by the Christian community.

Christ has already reached the end for ever. In him a single member of humanity has already arrived. The rest of humanity, the rest of creation, now feel an upward attraction towards the future, along with an impulse or a push. It is the attraction of the glory of Christ, the impulse of the spirit, like a wind which fills the sails to drive the ship towards its transfiguration. It is as if the ship had left a meridian of darkness and was transfigured in luminous clarity through the action of the sun that is already risen. Subjected to the two forces, it is being transformed from within, even if 'what we will be has not yet been revealed' (1 Jn 3:2).

It is as if the bread and wine have reached the longed-for end before us. They have done it, as the

Book of Wisdom says, for our salvation. Already transformed themselves, they insert in us a principle of gradual transfiguration which will progressively come to the definitive transformation. 'And all of us... are being transformed into the same image, from glory to glory, according to the action of the Spirit of the Lord' (2 Cor 3:18). We too long for this glorification to which we are called. The Eucharist is the testimony, guarantee and anticipation of our transformation. Even the community is being progressively transformed into a community of brothers and sisters, sons and daughters of God.

The Eucharist, as an articulated unity, is transformation. From the abundant repertoire of our tradition we can select a few categories: change, mutation, transformation, becoming, being made, refashioning, sanctification, consecration, transfiguration, reform – different words for the one mystery.

(N.B. I have barely touched upon one aspect of a complex and debated subject. For this reason I recommend the reader to the excellent historical and systematic exposition of Gesteira, *op. cit.*, pp. 421-574).

10. SACRIFICE

On the Eucharist as sacrifice there has been fervent investigation and discussion and countless writings. These seem to be necessary because of the importance of the subject and the difficulty of explaining the way in which the Eucharist is sacrifice. There is the question of the relationship between the many celebrations, all of them and each one of them, with the unique and unrepeatable sacrifice of Christ on the Cross.

My intention is modest, namely, to offer a few biblical reflections on the theme, to enrich our participation.

1. The Israelite community developed a complex and varied cultic system, which gave rise to a terminology just as varied. In the first place we must distinguish between sacrifice and offering (*zebah* and *minha*). In the former an animal was offered as victim, in the latter there was offered bread or flour, prepared in different ways and accompanied according to the circumstances by oil, salt or wine. Starting from the Offertory, our gifts are nearer to the 'offerings' than to the sacrifice. The word *minha* means tribute, that is, the offering of the vassal to the sovereign; it is at the same time both an act of recognition and of contribution. Our gifts can only express recognition; they cannot bring anything to God. The word *zebah* signifies killing an animal to eat it, and the noun can mean a banquet. This aspect appears in our Eucharistic banquet.

Another important distinction exists between holocaust and communion sacrifice (*'ôla* and *zebah shelamim*). In the first the whole victim is burnt (*'ôla* comes from the root *'lh* = go up: either because it goes up onto the altar, or because it goes up on high in the form of smoke or aroma?). The ashes were placed in a special refuse area. In the communion sacrifice a portion belonged to the Lord. The blood flowed around the altar, the fat and other parts were burnt, the meat was roasted and divided among the participants or guests at the sacred banquet. Our Eucharist reproduces elements of both types. The total offering of Christ to the Father is like a holocaust. Metaphorically, 'he is burnt out' and goes up like fragrance to the Father. In his death, freely accepted, he is 'burnt'; starting from it he will go up to the Father having been glorified (ascension = go up = *'ôla*). Beginning with this glorification he can communicate himself to his own in the sacred meal. Our Eucharist opens up into a banquet, and in this respect it comes quite close to the communion sacrifices of the Old Testament.

Both types of sacrifice are offered in different circumstances and for various reasons. There is, for example, the covenant sacrifice. It is a communion sacrifice and a holocaust. The blood is divided and sprinkled on the altar and on the people. The meat is eaten as a sacred banquet. Hence the expression 'the covenant sealed with a sacrifice' (Ps 50). Our Eucharist is explicitly a sacrifice of the 'new covenant', sealed with the blood of Christ and authenticated with the banquet of his body and blood which makes us table-companions of God. Sacrifices were also offered for the 'atonement for sins'. The most important was that which is offered on the Day of

Atonement (*yom kippur*). Our Eucharist mentions it explicitly: 'It will be shed for you and for all so that sins may be forgiven'. The penitential liturgy is linked to the Eucharistic banquet. It comes before it, because no one who is blemished may sit down at this table. Moreover, the shared banquet ratifies the reconciliation. Still another purpose of the banquet can be thanksgiving (Lev 7:12f). It is obvious that the Eucharist comes into this group, as its name indicates, that is, thanksgiving (*beraka*).

Although it is not a sacrifice, it is worth remembering at this point the offering of the first fruits (Deut 26). Since Christ is the first-fruit of creation, the first-born of humanity and those risen from the dead (see 1 Cor 15:20; Rom 8:29; Col 1:15.18), it follows that in the Eucharist we offer the Father our absolute first-fruit.

The plurality of cult in the Old Testament helps to illuminate different aspects of our celebration.

2. The whole of this institution is in some way relativized by another series of texts which deepen its meaning or transfer it to other acts.

First of all there is human sacrifice, known in antiquity and in various cultures. The Old Testament is categorically opposed to human sacrifices (usually, of first-born babies,'first-fruits of virility'); Lev 20:2; Deut 12:30f; 2 Kings 16:3; 17:31; 23:20; Ps 106:37f; Jer 7:30ff; 19:3ff; Ez 16:20; Wis 12:4f. The so-called sacrifice of Isaac puts this unanimous condemnation into relief. Legally, he is the first-born. The rite will be carried out in the prescribed way, that is, the victim is offered up and then burnt on the pyre, a complete holocaust for God. Does God refuse it? He replaces it with an animal. So God accepts as a sacrifice from Abraham what he wanted, that is, the submission and personal offering of the patriarch. As for its external expression, it is consumed as an animal victim. Human sacrifices are definitively abolished.

Furthermore, Tradition is unanimous in applying this passage to the Father and to Christ, as if God had accepted in the end what he had once refused, a human sacrifice. One must read this with critical detachment. If the death of Christ is a sacrifice, it does not follow cultic ritual; it even contradicts it. A 'criminal' hanged on the gibbet is abominable to God (Deut 21:23). The form seems to be a point by point negation of the ritual – not the temple, but the hill of executions, not an altar, but an ignominious cross, not an animal, but a condemned man; still less is there burning or a banquet. With such a denial of the ritual the authentic meaning of sacrifice seems to be saved, that is, the recognition and the offering.

I do not intend to talk here about the polemic of the prophets against sacrifices offered in a context of injustice or its consequences. I select two classical texts which attempt to correct and enlarge the meaning of sacrifice. One is Psalm 51, which ought to be explained in unity with the preceding psalm, as two moments of a penitential liturgy (see my book *Treinta Salmos,* pp. 189-230). I take three verses from it:

> 50:14 My sacrifice is to confess my sin.
> 23 To confess one's sin is the sacrifice which honours me.
> 51:19 The sacrifice acceptable to God is a broken heart.

Through confession in repentance the persons humble themselves before God, who accepts this profound attitude as a valid sacrifice which gives him honour. Of the Paschal victim one must not 'break' any bone. A spirit or conscience that is 'broken or contrite' is a sacrifice that God accepts. Christ cannot confess his own sins, he can put himself in solidarity with human sinners and offer himself in mercy for them. It is an offering that can have sacrificial value, according to the texts cited.

Psalm 40 offers us some verses which are commented on in the Epistle to the Hebrews 10:5-10:

> Ps 40:6 Sacrifice and offering thou dost not desire;
> but thou hast given me an open ear.
> Burnt offering and sin offering thou hast not required.
> 7 Then I said, 'Lo, I come;
> in the roll of the book it is written of me;
> 8 I delight to do thy will, O my God;
> thy law is within my heart'.

The full acceptance of the concrete plan of God in his person is equivalent to a sacrifice of himself. It substitutes with profit for holocausts, sacrifices and offerings. The total offering of Christ to the plan of the Father to the point of death, even death on the cross, is sacrificial in a profound sense, and can profitably abolish and replace all the preceding sacrifices. Now, we offer this oblation of Christ to the Father as the Eucharistic sacrifice. We can unite ourselves to it only if we take the plan of God on ourselves, sacrificing even our rooted interest and egoism.

It is not hard to associate this text with the one we mentioned about Abraham, and also with the classical quote of Samuel to Saul (1 Sam 15,22) 'Obedience is worth far more than a sacrifice, to be submissive is better than the fat of rams'. The difference lies in the fact that Psalm 40 does not make comparisons or, if it does, it is to affirm the profound meaning of some practices that are already surpassed.

3. *From our culture.* This element is not, strictly speaking, biblical, even though it agrees with an aspect of the thought of Israel. In many modern languages a 'sacrifice' means any renunciation which a person makes for a higher value. It is frequently used when referring to the good of others.

The Oxford English Dictionary defines it as, 'the destruction or surrender of something valued or desired for the sake of something having a higher or more pressing claim; the loss entailed by devotion to some other interest'. A first reaction can consider such a use to be a secularization of the sacred. It is called sacri-fice without being sacred... But attentive reflection permits us to discover a quite precious aspect of the sacrifice of Christ and his eucharistic celebration.

In effect, it was not just a question of a formality in submitting himself to the plan of the Father, whatever that was. The content also mattered. The plan of the Father is that his Son should sacrifice himself for men and women: 'for us and for our salvation he came down from heaven, suffered and died'.

The Old Testament knows the idea of an innocent person who suffers for the sake of others and for their benefit (Is 53), but it does not call this 'sacrifice'. But the Epistle to the Hebrews, which deals at great length with the Jewish and Christian cult, exhorts:

Heb 13:15 Through Jesus Christ let us continually offer up a sacrifice of praise to God, that is, the fruit of lips that acknowledge his name.

16 Do not neglect to do good and to share what you have, for such sacrifices are pleasing to God.

The lips which 'bless' (*beraka*) 'offer a sacrifice of praise', and to do good is a 'sacrifice' in which God delights. There is here a notable concentration of cultic language. We cannot minimize the matter with the excuse that we are dealing with metaphor, because it can happen that this Christian practice merits the name sacrifice better than purely ritual practices.

I believe that this aspect — sacrifice for the neighbour — united with other more biblical aspects, can help us understand the Eucharist as sacrifice.

4. *The two moments.* In every sacrifice we can see a moment of destruction and another of exaltation. There is the burning followed by the rising of fragrance on high, renouncing something good and seeing it accepted by the one whom we hold in high esteem, sacrificing oneself and seeing oneself consecrated or taking something from a human sphere and interest and seeing it transferred into the divine sphere.

The primary thing is the reality and its expression. The Israelite slits the throat of the victim and burns it on the wood of the altar. In this way he expresses his nothingness before God, recognizing that his whole being comes from, depends on and is from God. It is not something he possesses, it is himself – or a self which he possesses through consciousness and freedom. He gives himself as an interior holocaust which is expressed in the real holocaust of the offered victim. The human being experiences him/herself as 'dust and ash' (Gen

18:27; Job 30:19; 42:6), the dust which he/she was before becoming a human being, the ash in which the burning ends. In this spiritual reducing of oneself to dust and ash, the human being opens himself/herself to transcendence and is led to God, like the victim accepted in the form of aroma (*reh nihoh:* Gen 8:21; frequently in Leviticus and Numbers).

Humankind, a human community, looks for stable relations with the divinity. Or better, God hastens to offer himself to them. God commits himself freely and sovereignly. Humankind accepts freely. An agreement will be stipulated or signed. Human beings put their lives at the disposal and at the service of God, the life which is in the blood. They express this by sprinkling and offering the blood of a victim. God receives it and consecrates it, and with it signs the two parts. He signs the altar, which is his exclusive table, and he signs the people by sprinkling them (Ex 24:5-8). In a loud voice the document of the covenant is read, its acceptance is proclaimed, and the covenant is sealed with the blood of the sacrifice. In the new covenant this function is fulfilled by the blood of Christ which is offered to the Father on the Cross and to men and women in the Eucharist.

The 'ally' of God wants to be the host and the guest of God. To this end he 'sacrifices' some precious possession, for example, one of his beasts. He cancels in some way its useful value, renounces its possession, and offers it generously to the divinity who accepts it. At this point it remains consecrated and cannot be assigned to profane use. Here the will is more important than the gift, because God will not feed on such offerings, 'Will I eat the flesh of bulls, will I drink the blood of goats?' (Ps 50:13). Accepting with pleasure the will and the gesture of the person, God establishes communication or communion. In this sense he becomes the invited guest of the human being. God does not eat, or rather, he is nourished of himself, because his being is fullness without limit. (We can note that even the human spirit can nourish and enrich itself by its thinking, feeling and willing.) Even the human being can be a table-guest of God, as a result of having invited God. This can happen only through a communication-communion of God which is expressed by the invitation to the banquet of the sacrificed victim.

In the New Testament the communion sacrifice is the Eucharist. There is a human renunciation of the 'gifts' as its expression. There is above all a total renunciation by Christ as the victim. Only by passing through this moment can Christ communicate his new consecrated life, and he does so by consecrating the goods offered. Here the moment of glorification returns. This glorification is the moment that corresponds to the annihilation which is death. Further it is the condition for giving us his life, which was impossible before. 'How can this man gives us his flesh to eat?... This way of speaking is intolerable: who can listen to it?' (Jn 6:52.60). The glorification is like an apex, corresponding with the death and corresponding with some of the gifts.

Participating at the banquet, the community too is consecrated. Renouncing its purely biological life, it can share in the life of Christ and become Christian. This is the communion sacrifice.

5. *Liturgical formulae.* Let us now run through some of the texts of the new liturgy, to see how this aspect is formulated.

Common to all, as part of this so-called Offertory, is this invitation and reply:

> Pray, brethren, that my sacrifice and yours may be acceptable to God, the almighty Father.
> May the Lord accept the sacrifice at your hands for the praise and glory of his name, for our good, and the good of all his Church.

Twice it speaks of sacrifice. It mentions the offering and the acceptance. It expresses its double purpose (with allusion to the covenant) for God and for men and women, and it affirms its ecclesial significance.

All the following formulae, referring expressly to the death and resurrection, or to the paschal mystery, imply the theme of sacrifice.

The first Preface of the Eucharist summarizes the essentials with remarkable precision:

> He is the true and eternal priest
> who established this unending sacrifice.
> He offered himself as a victim for our deliverance
> and taught us to make this offering in his memory.
> As we eat his body which he gave for us,
> we grow in strength.
> As we drink his blood which he poured out for us,
> we are washed clean.

This first Anaphora asks God 'to accept and bless these gifts we offer you in sacrifice' [Latin: *Uti acceptas habeas et benedicas haec dona, haec munera, haec sancta sacrificia illibata*], and repeats it in an affirmative formula after the institution narrative: 'this holy and perfect sacrifice: the bread of life and the cup of eternal salvation' [Latin: *Hostiam pu-*

ram..., panem sanctum vitae eternae et calicem salutis perpetuae].

The second Anaphora expresses it in a different way, which will be clear following the previous discussion:

> He opened his arms on the cross... In this he fulfilled your will... Before he was given up to death, a death he freely accepted... [Latin: *Qui cum Passioni voluntariae traderetur*].

The third Anaphora has:

> We offer you in thanksgiving
> this holy and living sacrifice.
> ...Look with favour on your Church's offering,
> and see the Victim whose death has reconciled us to yourself.

And the fourth Anaphora:

> In fulfilment of your will
> he gave himself up to death;
> but by rising from the dead,
> he destroyed death and restored life.
> ...We offer you his body and blood,
> the acceptable sacrifice... [Latin: *Sacrificium tibi acceptabile*].

It is special to this Eucharistic Prayer to unite as two victims Christ and his Church:

> Lord, look upon this sacrifice [Latin: *Hostia*]
> which you have given [Latin: *Parasti*] to your Church;
> and by your Holy Spirit,
> gather all who share this one bread and one cup
> into the one body of Christ,
> a living sacrifice of praise [Latin: *Hostia viva perficiantur, ad laudem gloriae tuae*].

Here resonates the teaching of the Epistle to the Hebrews referred to above.

The Eucharistic sacrifice we celebrate impresses on us the meaning of sacrifice which the Christian life has, in its double dimension of renunciation and consecration.

6. It is now time to gather together and complete all that has been said.

The sacrifice of Christ is the total stripping of himself in order to offer himself entirely to the Father. 'Not my will but yours.' To be complete, the offering must include death. One does not seek death to put to the test (Wis 2:19-20); one accepts death as the test of love. 'No one has a greater love than he who gives his life for his friends.' To accept a plan of the Father which includes death is a total stripping of self. Blotting himself out, he offers himself entirely to the Father, as in sacrifice (Ps 40). Accepting it, the Father transforms it: by introducing it into the divine sphere? But Christ already belongs there. By divinizing humanity? But the natures are not confused nor are they transformed. The Father transforms it by glorifying humanity through the resurrection. The sacrifice consecrates in so far as it goes up in a new way to the sacred, divine sphere.

We recognize that we receive everything from God, right to the root of our being. Inasmuch as we receive being from the Other, we are and we exist. Now, in so far as we are persons we possess our being. We know it and we freely realize it. To recognize our total debt of gratitude we strip ourselves of it, not to annihilate ourselves which would not honour God, but renouncing our possession of ourselves, so that we can be totally possessed by the giver. This is sacrificing ourselves. When God accepts it, he transfers it to the divine sphere, he consecrates it.

To express our stripping-sacrifice, we deprive ourselves of useful things and offer them to God. We deprive ourselves of their use and consumption; we cancel their useful value and refill them with meaning and expression. We offer them in the way that we can sacrifice our flowers to adorn a festival. The 'loaves of the presence' in time of scarcity meant, 'to take the bread out of one's mouth'. If God accepts our offerings, he con-secrates or sacri-fices them, he raises them up to his own sphere. How does God accept them? Not naturally, since he neither eats nor drinks (Ps 50). He accepts them as a valid expression, and can use symbols which indicate the acceptance – by consuming them in the fire, which is a divine element. He accepts them in the form of fragrance, which is less material than food, closer to the living breath, to respiration, like incense transformed into fragrance in being burnt. However the Christian community which is the Body of Christ goes beyond all our offerings and in a different order of things offers once again to the Father the sacrifice of his Son, the total offering, the sacrifice for love, the death, and glorification. And it is offered for the plan of the Father, through the Christian life in fraternal love.

11. COMMUNION

We are accustomed to call 'communion' the act of taking, receiving or swallowing the eucharistic bread and wine, as an essential part of a banquet. From all that has been proposed in the preceding reflections, we can conclude that this interpretation is true, but a little restricted. The communion can be a moment, an act of the Eucharist, but we can also consider it as an aspect. That is how I will explain it, using the following categories: communion, communication, participation and sharing.

For this let us begin by reading a story about Elijah (1 Kings 17:10-16):

> Elijah arose and went to Zarephath; and when he came to the gate of the city, behold, a widow was there gathering sticks; and he called to her and said, 'Bring me a little water in a vessel, that I may drink'. And as she was going to bring it, he called to her and said, 'Bring me a morsel of bread in your hand'. And she said, 'As the Lord your God lives, I have nothing baked, only a handful of meal in a jar, and a little oil in a cruse; and now I am gathering a couple of sticks, that I may go in and prepare it for myself and my son, that we may eat it, and die'. And Elijah said to her, 'Fear not; go and do as you have said; but first make me a little cake of it and bring it to me, and afterwards make for yourself and your son.' For thus says the Lord the God of Israel, 'The jar of meal shall not be spent, and the cruse of oil shall not fail, until the day that the Lord sends rain upon the earth.' And she went and did as Elijah said. And she, and he, and her household ate for many days. The jar of meal was not spent, neither did the cruse of oil

fail, according to the word of the Lord which he spoke by Elijah.

The widow and her son are about to divide their last mouthfuls – the meal of two people condemned to death. Elijah asks that first they share what they have with a stranger who can only offer them a divine oracle. Does Elijah want to accelerate death or prolong their life? The widow listens to the oracle as the word of God, she trusts in the promise and divides the one last piece of food that remains, sharing much more than the widow's mite of which the Gospel speaks.

It is a supreme example of sharing; not only a few handfuls of flour and a jug of oil, but in these her life and that of her son. The three were already sharing the same faith and hope in God, and they will continue to share the word-promise of God made bread and oil.

A story reduced to the bare essentials, it could be enough for a meditation on eucharistic communion. Jesus offers and shares right up to the end his life and his blood, to enable us to share in his glorified life. But we must also participate in his word, in order to share it then as bread.

2. To share is to give to another a part of my own, or to apportion something among various persons, even without dividing it. The Israelites shared many things. In the first place the promised land is delivered and distributed by lot by Joshua. To each family must belong its share or fixed portion of land, so that the participation of all in the land which is the gift of God becomes a reality and is perpetuated. But there are greedy speculators 'who add house to house, and unite field to field, until there is no more

space and they remain alone to inhabit the land' (Is 5:8). They do not share and they do not communicate; they are condemned to solitude.

And those who do not receive an hereditary portion, the immigrants, the Levites? With the fruits of the earth one must provide for their necessity, 'I have taken from my house what was consecrated to God, and I have given it to the Levite, to the stranger, to the orphan and the widow, according to all that you have commanded me' (Deut 6:13). What about the poor? With loans and alms, even they must participate in the goods of the earth: 'Open generously your hand to your poor and needy brother in your land' (Deut 15:11).

The Israelites shared the same fathers, Abraham, Isaac and Jacob, and the same history which begins with the liberation from Egypt. They recount it and sing it in common. They shared the joy of the national festivals, but also the weight of sins, which they confessed in common. Thus, they shared responsibilities and tasks. Nehemiah will assign to each family or group a section of the walls of Jerusalem so that they may reconstruct the city in common.

The Israelites shared the same king from the time of David. Yet disputes could still arise as to who had the greatest right to the king:

2 Sam 19:41 Then all the men of Israel came to the king, and said to the king, 'Why have our brethren the men of Judah stolen you away, and brought the king and his household over the Jordan, and all David's men with him?'

42 All the men of Judah answered the men of Israel, 'Because the king is near of kin to us. Why then are you angry over this matter? Have we eaten at all at the king's expense? Or has he given us any gift?'

43 And the men of Israel answered the men of Judah, 'We have ten shares in the king, and in David also we have more than you. Why then did you despise us?'

When the schism occurred, the cry of rebellion sounded like this:

1 Kings 12:16 What portion have we in David?
We have no inheritance in the son of Jesse.

The Israelites shared the same God, whom they called the Lord our God. 'Do we not all have one father? Has not one God created us' (Mal 2:10). Against this broad background, which we could amplify, should be read particular cases.

3. These particular cases will be texts in which there appears the theme of the banquet or the meal as an expression of participation or sharing.

In the first text we seem to be attending a proto-Eucharist. A protagonist expounds the recent deeds of God the saviour and liberator and the priest replies with a blessing (*beraka*) to the Lord for his benefits. Victims are offered in sacrifice and a communion banquet is celebrated:

Ex 18:8-12 Then Moses told his father-in-law all that the Lord had done to Pharaoh and to the Egyptians for Israel's sake, all the hardship that had come upon them on the way, and how the Lord had delivered them. And Jethro rejoiced for all the good which the Lord had done to Israel, in that he had delivered them out of the hand of the Egyptians. And Jethro said, 'Blessed be the Lord, who has delivered you out of the hand of the Egyptians and out of the hand of Pharaoh. Now I know that the Lord is greater than all gods, because he delivered the people from under the hand of the Egyptians, when they dealt arrogantly with them'. And

Jethro, Moses' father-in-law, offered a burnt offering and sacrifices to God; and Aaron came with all the elders of Israel to eat bread with Moses' father-in-law before God.

It begins as a family affair. The wife and sons who are living with the father and the grandfather Jethro, go out to welcome Moses. At the end representatives of Israel participate in the sacrificial banquet.

Less evocative, and more communitarian, is the episode in which David has the Ark brought to Jerusalem. The narrator is very interested in the king's liturgical dance, and limits himself to a brief report about the rest.

2 Sam 6:17 And they brought in the ark of the Lord, and set it in its place, inside the tent which David had pitched for it; and David offered burnt offerings and peace offerings before the Lord.

18 And when David had finished offering the burnt offerings and the peace offerings, he blessed the people in the name of the Lord of hosts,

19 and distributed among all the people, the whole multitude of Israel, both men and women, to each a cake of bread, a portion of meat, and a cake of raisins.

Besides the sacrificial character of a banquet, we see here its festive character and the royal bounty. All must make merry on that festive day, and their joy will be expressed in their equal participation in a substantial meal provided by the king. The blessing of the people is in the nature of a conclusion; it is not the blessing of thanksgiving to God.

4. On top of these two episodes there comes a memory which has nourished religious fantasy and theological reflection in the Old and New Tes-

taments. We are speaking about manna. A food given prodigiously in the desert, and little appreciated by its immediate beneficiaries (Num 11); it was transformed in the poetic vision of the late Book of Wisdom:

16:20 Instead of these things thou didst give thy people the food of angels,
and without their toil thou didst supply them from heaven with bread ready to eat,
providing every pleasure and suited to every taste.

21 For thy sustenance manifested thy sweetness toward thy children;
and the bread, ministering to the desire of the one who took it,
was changed to suit everyone's liking.

An important reference in the Gospel of John (6:31,49) and three other allusions (1 Cor 10:3; Heb 9:4; Rev 2:17) have secured for the manna the value of a symbol or type, thanks to which it passed into Christian tradition and was successful in theology and spirituality. I will dwell on this aspect of nourishment, since the manna is not a banquet, nor is it linked with the cult and sacrifices. However it represents quite well the equalitarian and provisional character of the product.

We begin with its communitarian and equalitarian character:

Ex 16:15-18 Moses said to them, 'It is the bread which the Lord has given you to eat'. This is what the Lord has commanded: 'Gather of it, every man of you, as much as he can eat; you shall take an omer apiece, according to the number of persons whom each of you has in his tent'. And the people of Israel did so; they gathered, some more, some less. But when they measured it with an omer, he that gathered much had nothing over, and he that gathered little had no lack; each gathered according to what he could eat.

The bread 'which God makes rain from heaven' is enough to satisfy the needs of everyone; it does not serve to create rich and poor. It is a gift of God, heavenly rain, and the people need only harvest it.

Its provisional character links it with the Sabbath obligation:

Es 16:19-26 And Moses said to them, 'Let no man leave any of it till the morning'. But they did not listen to Moses; some left part of it till the morning, and it bred worms and became foul; and Moses was angry with them. Morning by morning they gathered it, each as much as he could eat; but when the sun grew hot, it melted. On the sixth day they gathered twice as much bread, two omers apiece; and when all the leaders of the congregation came and told Moses. He said to them, 'This is what the Lord has commanded: "Tomorrow is a day of solemn rest, a holy sabbath to the Lord; bake what you will bake and boil what you will boil, and all that is left over lay by to be kept till the morning"'. So they laid it by till the morning, as Moses bade them; and it did not become foul, and there were no worms in it. Moses said, 'Eat it today, for today is a sabbath to the Lord; today you will not find it in the field.'

Each day they gathered and consumed the daily ration. On Friday they also gathered the ration for the next day, which is the day of rest. This point brings us to the Our Father which we recite before Communion. An enigmatic Greek adjective, *epiousion*, has sometimes been translated 'daily', and other times 'supersubstantial'. An ancient Semitic tradition understood it as 'imminent, of tomorrow'. This gives us two readings which are in accord with our Eucharist. It is the bread of every day and the bread of tomorrow. In other words, it is the daily bread of our pilgrimage, and the bread of the heavenly tomorrow which is anticipated in order to nourish us with the future immortal life. This is because tomorrow is the day of rest, definitve rest which is anticipated in our weekly celebration of the day of the Lord.

5. Another favourite text from Tradition is Wisdom's banquet presented in Proverbs 9. Wisdom or learning appears personified as a noble lady who gives an invitation to a banquet. Chapter 9 closes the initial section of the book and introduces to what follows. In this way the remainder of the book is like the rich and varied banquet laid for pleasure and nourishment.

Pr 9:1 Wisdom has built her house,
she has set up her seven pillars.
2 She has slaughtered her beasts, she has mixed her wine,
she has also set her table.
3 She has sent out her maids to call
from the highest places in the town,
4 'Whoever is simple, let him turn in here!'
To him who is without sense she says,
5 'Come, eat of my bread
and drink of the wine I have mixed.
6 Leave simpleness, and live,
and walk in the way of insight.'

Even the Wisdom of Sirach 24 invites with her fruits:

Sir 24:19 Come to me, you who desire me,
and eat your fill of my produce.
20 For the remembrance of me is sweeter than honey,
and my inheritance sweeter than the honeycomb.
21 Those who eat me will hunger for more,
and those who drink me will thirst for more.

Since Paul has called Christ the 'Wisdom of God' (1 Cor 1:30), tradition over the centuries has applied the two quoted texts to Christ, referring them especially to the Eucharist. He offers us his paradoxical and superior wisdom, and offers it to us as consummate wisdom. There is something in this last datum to reflect on.

6. *The Eucharistic banquet.* I hope that it may now be possible to broaden our vision. One of the aims of the recent liturgical reform was to encourage participation. Participating and sharing are our guide-words. 'To celebrate' the Mass, and not only to hear it, to communicate, and not just to assist. Sharing reaches its high point in the communion, but it is not limited to it.

The community first share the readings and listening to the word of God. Long ago Augustine observed the fact of a one word which sounds in one person's mouth, distributing itself without being divided, reaching everyone in an equal way, and through convergence creating a circle of attention. Everyone shares the bread of the word, each according to their needs and capability, neither too much for one, nor too little for another. In the sharing they strengthen their unity. The word is not the monopoly of a few chosen people (as could have been the impression when the readings were done in Latin). In the readings we are offered that wisdom and learning of Christ which must fashion our Christian thinking and feeling. Rather than uniform theories, we need to assimilate the learning of the gospel, each and every one of us, so that it comes to be our Christian 'common sense'. It is a process that has its privileged moment in the Eucharist.

Responding to the proclamation, we can recite in agreement our profession of faith and sing in unison or harmony our common sentiment. (Even the counterpoint could be presented as a model of unity in the variety of voices.) Is there a better model of the unity desired than music? There is a score: each sings his/her own part, one directs, and the entire space that surrounds us adapts and moulds the vibrations which joyfully invade us, transporting us with their sound into the world of the spirit. Even silent listening to an instrumental piece can unite and mould us all.

In the Eucharistic celebration there is another paradoxical communion, and that is the confession of sins. Apart from the burden of sins which each person carries, there are the shared faults of the community. We have seen how the Israelites felt united in the confession of common sins. In fact, to confess in this way is to accept common and shared responsibility. If we share a responsibility, we also share jointly in the consequent errors. If there were common responsibilities in the past, they will be there in the future too, for they are the community obligations. The Eucharist can develop in us this communitarian sense.

For the Communion in the strict sense, it will be enough to gather up some of the things we have already said or alluded to. One flesh is divided for all (as did David at the feast of the Ark); one blood circulates in the body of the community, carrying the oxygen of the Spirit to every cell. It is like the air which surrounds us and which we breathe: it comes out in the form of words and spreads its vibrations, a mediator of verbal communication. It is like the light which surrounds us and acts upon us: reflecting itself it reveals our personal profile and is the mediator of our presence to one another. So the glorified body of Christ becomes a means of communication and communion. Does he enter into us? Or rather do we enter into him? With this reality we overcome our shared memory without blotting it out.

Through this mysterious communion, all is communion in the Eucharist.

7. The texts are not too generous in proposing or explaining this aspect. It is as though what had finally ensued after the word was action and silence. The text for this part of the Eucharist is sober: the Our Father and what follows, the Sign of Peace, the presentation of the 'Lamb of God' and the words of the centurion. Some would think that it is rushed. It would be better to say that it calms down into silence. Even silence can be shared as a fullness, since all are 'filled with the Lord, as the waters fill the sea' (Is 11:9).

I would like to choose some relevant texts from the Proper of the Missal.

From the Second Sunday in Ordinary time:

> Lord,
> you have nourished us with bread from heaven.
> Fill us with your Spirit,
> and make us one in peace and love.

From the Fifth Sunday:

> God our Father,
> you give us a share in the one bread and the one cup
> and make us one in Christ.
> Help us to bring your salvation and joy
> to all the world.

From the Eleventh Sunday:

> Lord,
> may this eucharist

accomplish in your Church
the unity and peace it signifies.

From the Twenty-sixth Sunday:

Lord,
may this eucharist
in which we proclaim the death of Christ
bring us salvation
and make us one with him in glory,
for he is Lord for ever and ever.

It appears significant to me that it is precisely in the liturgy for Christian Unity that we find such meaningful texts on communion and union. It prays that we 'may form one family in the bond of love and in true faith', that we may work 'to unite all believers in the bond of peace', that 'overcoming all division among Christians, your Church may be formed again in perfect communion'. A post-communion prayer speaks thus:

Grant that this eucharistic communion,
sign of our fraternity in Christ,
may make your Church holy with the bond of love.

Aware that union is a duty, one prayer asks for the gift of the Spirit 'so that with sincere searching and common commitment we may rebuild the perfect unity of your family'. One of the Entrance Antiphons recalls the classic text from the Letter to the Ephesians (4:4-6):

There is one body, one spirit,
as one only is the hope to which we are called;
one Lord, one faith, one baptism,
one God and Father of all,
who is above all, among all and in all.

8. The communion of the Eucharist continues in the present and in the future. In the present, since we must be a community in order that there may be communion, because we must share many goods before sharing the body and blood of Christ. In the future, because the Eucharistic communion is an example and impulse for continuing in the sharing and in the communion.

In the final instance, it is egoism that hinders us and makes it difficult to share and communicate. We hang on to goods we possess, even spiritual ones; we close in on ourselves. Today we have many means of communication. Does communication between people increase in proportion? At best these means only communicate information to us; they can even prevent people communicating with each other. In the end we are smothered, buried in data, to the point of being deprived of communication.

It is true that communicating information is a way of sharing, because information can be precious, but it is not everything. It is true that a spontaneous modesty impels us to hide our interiority. For this reason the communication of our intimate self is so much more precious.

Eucharistic communion can be a school of communication. We share the glorified body and blood of Christ because the Father has communicated to us his Son, a person, not simply information. 'He did not spare his own Son, but gave him up for us all. Will he not give us all things with him?' (Rom 8:32). Furthermore, the Father communicates to us the Son, who is communication, because in God all is communication of the totality of being, and the communication of being is the being or consistency of the persons. The Father, making us share in his Son, gives us the example and the capacity to communicate:

Jn 14:20 In that day you will know that I am in my Father, and you in me, and I in you.

17:21 Even as thou, Father, art in me, and I in thee, that they also may be one in us.

12. THE FINAL BLESSING

1. Our Eucharist ends with a new sign of the cross and a new trinitarian invocation which form an important inclusion. But this time, at the end of the celebration, the meaning is different. It is not an identifying mark but a blessing.

For this reason we must remember all we have said about 'blessing' in connection with the offertory = ***beraka***. When a person 'blesses' God, he/she gives recognition and thanks. When God blesses the people, he pronounces an efficacious word, and grants good things. In other words, God has communicated by blessing the person with the fruits of the earth; the person replies by offering a pleasing gift, the fruit of his/her work. God responds by blessing the person again. Such is the rhythm of the great dialogue.

To understand it better, I would like to quote and comment on Psalm 134 as a model. It deals with the changing of the priestly service in the temple. Day and night the turns of duty follow on one another in the house of the Lord. Through the priests, its representatives, the people come and stand in the presence of the Lord. Perhaps the different acts of service are less important, looking after the candelabra and the lamps, replacing the bread, watching at the door. It is probably more important that they represent a community which is a guest in the land of the Lord and wants to be in the house of the Lord: 'Blessed is the one you have chosen and called near, to dwell in your courts' (Ps 65:5).

The turns of duty are assigned to the priestly families, so as to keep the rhythm going and ensure continuity: 'all day and all night they will never be silent' (Is 62:6). Those who are finishing hand over to those coming in:

Is 62:6 Come, bless the Lord,
all you servants of the Lord,
who stand by night in the house of the Lord!
Lift up your hands towards the holy place
and bless the Lord.
May the Lord bless you from Zion,
he who made both heaven and earth!

The role of the priests is to 'bless the Lord', that is, to thank him in the name of the community for all his benefits and blessings. While neighbours and citizens sleep, their hearts are awake in the persons of the priests. Their hands, raised towards the sanctuary, or towards the building which rises within the great court of the temple, raise and present the community. It is like the arms of Moses which were held up in intercession (Ex 17:11f). God has begun to bless his people, and the people respond by blessing God. Thus unfolds the great dialogue between the people and their God. It is no small matter to be the interlocutors in such noble proceedings.

The dialogue does not end here. God, who has the first word, also has the last. For this reason the Psalm adds a verse with an efficacious request. Someone, perhaps the leader of the group, asks the Lord for a blessing (like another epiclesis). Will the dialogue continue in this way? It does, with an important difference. The person, blessing God, pronounces words, 'speaks well' (cf. *bene-diction*). He expresses sentiments, but he does not realize or carry them out. But when God blesses, he pronounces efficacious words. In speaking well, he benefits, his blessing is a beneficience. In the beginning he spoke words and 'created the heaven and the earth'. The one who, by giving an order created the universe, can with his blessing preserve and enrich his people.

Here we have the rhythm of our Eucharist. At the end, he who made the heaven and the earth, he who transformed the fruits of the earth in the glorified body of his Son, blesses us. With what blessings?

2. Before replying, I would like to round off the Psalm I quoted by adding a couple of texts. I take the first from Psalm 138, which ends with a most beautiful utterance. The psalm opens as the thanksgiving of the person praying, to which the other people must unite:

Ps 138 1 I give thee thanks, O Lord, with my whole heart...
2 I bow down toward thy holy temple
and give thanks to thy name
for thy steadfast love and thy faithfulness.
4 All the kings of the earth shall praise thee, O Lord.

It is a eucharistic psalm. 'To give thanks' can sound like a synonym of 'to bless'. The one praying has received various benefits, 'On the day when I called to you, you answered'. 'You give me back my life... and your right hand has saved me'. It is right to be thankful for what has been done, and it is no less right to ask for what is lacking, since there is much that remains for the person to do, and much that remains for God to do. It is precisely this which the final exclamation asks for or expects:

> 8 The Lord will fulfil his purpose for me;
> thy steadfast love, O Lord, endures for ever.
> Do not forsake the work of thy hands.

While we are concluding our Eucharist or thanksgiving, is there anything else for God to do? His concluding blessing will be both the pledge that there is and the dynamism that will bring it about. What precedes is its guarantee and its source.

The second text is the ending of Psalm 90. It expresses the feeling of human transience and the brevity of life. It begs that our brief span of existence might be filled with meaning. Its intensity makes up for its brevity:

> 17 Let the favour of the Lord our God be upon us,
> and establish thou the work of our hands upon us,
> yea, the work of our hands establish thou it.

The rhythm of this psalm is quite different from the Eucharist, but its ending leads us to look at the content of the blessing.

3. What blessings are given to us? First of all, the blessings centred on the Eucharistic celebration. In the renewal of the sacrifice of Christ are concentrated all the blessings which God the Father has granted us through Christ, and which are referred to in the letter to the Ephesians:

> 1:3 Blessed be the God and Father of our Lord Jesus Christ, who has blessed us in Christ with every spiritual blessing in the heavenly places.

At the end of Mass there opens a door to make way for this inexhaustible accumulation of graces, to the power or energy of a glorified body. The door takes the form of a cross, and it opens with a trinitarian sound.

Speaking of graces and of gifts can give us a false or limited idea. The quantity of water delivered from a reservoir is not just a voluminous mass of matter, but energy which will become light, which will give power to factories, set machines going and fertilize fields... the biblical blessing belongs to the sphere of energy much more than to the sphere of matter.

The first chapter of Genesis, which arranges the work of creation in a scheme, recounts the creation of the animals:

Gen 1:21 So God created the great sea monsters and every living creature that moves, with which the waters swarm, according to their kinds, and every winged bird according to its kind.

24 And God said, 'Let the earth bring forth living creatures according to their kinds; cattle and creeping things and beasts of the earth according to their kinds'. And it was so.

25 And God made the beasts of the earth according to their kinds and the cattle according to their kinds, and everything that creeps along the ground according to its kind.

Why the monotonous or solemn insistence on 'according to their species'? Because the author impresses on us that in the beginning God did not create all the animals individually but only the first of the species. The same happened with human beings. In these animals, and in humankind, God infused the power of procreation as a participation in his creative power. This wonderful dynamism is taken up in the blessing:

Gen 1:22 God blessed them, saying, 'Be fruitful and multiply and fill the waters in the seas, and let birds multiply on the earth'.

28 And God blessed them, and God said to them,

'Be fruitful and multiply, and fill the earth and subdue it.'

The blessing is not principally a granting of gifts, but a granting of power. Fruitfulness is the first and greatest blessing. Every blessing of God has something of a genesis, but glorification exceeds Genesis.

When Eve saw herself to be the mother of a son, she exclaimed, 'I have given birth with the help of the Lord' (Gen 4:1). Eve is (means) Mother of the living.[1]

4. Fruitfulness implies above all generation:

Gen 5:1 When God created man, he made him in the likeness of God.
2 Male and female he created them, and he blessed them...
3 When Adam had lived a hundred and thirty years, he became the father of a son in his own likeness.

The human being generates a new human being, who is corporeal and spiritual. But the Spirit possesses other forms of fruitfulness, so we speak of a fruitful life, of a fruitful writer or composer. Such is the meaning of the conclusion of Psalm 90. Since our life fulfils itself in a series of deeds and enterprises, we invoke the blessing of God that he may render them fruitful. 'Make the work of our hands prosper.'

Some ask God to give them things already made, or that he do them himself. But it is normally more correct to ask God to make us capable of doing them. 'Our ability comes from God, he has equip-

---

[1] See the commentary in *¿Dónde está tu hermano?* (cit.), pp. 24-25.

ped us for the service of a new covenant' (1 Cor 3:5-6). 'Beware of thinking, that my strength and the might of my hand have gotten me this wealth. Remember instead the Lord your God, because he gives you the strength to acquire riches' (Deut 8:17f).

The weekly Eucharist (and the daily one) is a pause in our tasks. When we begin a new stage, we bow down to receive the blessing of God for our enterprises – bodily, intellectual, spiritual, individual or social. In the life of Israel, the series sounded like this:

Deut 28:3 Blessed shall you be in the city, and blessed shall you be in the field.
4 Blessed shall be the fruit of your body, and the fruit of your ground, and the fruit of your beasts, the increase of your cattle, and the young of your flock.
5 Blessed shall be your baskets and your kneading-trough.
6 Blessed shall you be when you come in, and blessed shall you be when you go out.

The series is sufficiently concrete to reflect a society and an economy, an urban and rural culture sufficiently stylized so as to function symbolically. The city and the countryside: the city is the *polis*, mother of politics as social intercourse. The countryside is the means of production in an organized chain. Both are the relationship between producing and consuming. Blessed be both and their relationship. Livestock is fruitful for food and clothing (cf. Prov 27:26f); they are wealth and they produce wealth. From *pecus* comes *pecunia*. Today we add the mechanical and intelligent fruitfulness of industry. The basket is for gathering, the kneading-trough for transformation. Is not the factory an ingenious kneading-trough for transformation? To go out is to begin, to enter is to conclude.

Naturally, blessings are not uniquely or principally material, to do with well-being. They are first of all blessings 'of the Spirit' for the Christian life.

5. Much less have blessings to do with individual interests and advantages; that would be to contradict the meaning of 'communion', of sharing.

The blessing which closes the Eucharist takes the form of a cross. Can the cross be a blessing? 'Cursed be he who hangs from the tree', says the Law (Deut 21:23). The letter to the Galatians replies:

> 3:13 Christ redeemed us from the curse of the law, having become a curse for us — for it is written,'Cursed be every one who hangs on a tree',
>
> 14 that in Christ Jesus the blessing of Abraham might come upon the Gentiles, that we might receive the promise of the Spirit through faith.

The cross in itself is not a blessing but an ignominious torture. But the sacrifice for love is fruitful. For this reason the cross of Christ is the fountain or river-bed of blessing. The form of the cross which the liturgy imprints at the blessing serves as a reminder that the fruitfulness that springs from the Eucharist passes through the sacrifice of egoism, and that the sacrifice and suffering for the service of others is the source of fruitfulness because it is blessed by God. Thus we connect with the beginning of the celebration, which signed us with this sign of salvation.

The blessing takes place invoking the name of the Trinity. The classical text of blessing in Israel, Numbers 6, offers a text and explains the ceremony:

23 Thus you shall bless the people of Israel:
24 'The Lord bless you and keep you.
25 The Lord make his face to shine upon you,
and be gracious to you.
26 The Lord lift up his countenance upon you,
and give you peace.
27 So shall they put my name upon the people of Israel, and I will bless them'.

Here blessing is strictly the action of God. The priests are invited to invoke the name of the Lord (a kind of epiclesis). The name is pronounced three times (we translate *Yhwh* by Lord, according to the traditional custom).

The invocation which closes the Eucharistic celebration is also made with the invocation of the name of God; not three times, but with the trinitarian name. 'May almighty God bless you, the Father, and Son, and the Holy Spirit.'

Day after day, week after week, our Christian life 'increases and multiplies', the effect of the repeated blessing. But the rhythm of existence must not make us forget hope: 'For this you have been called, so that you may inherit a blessing' (1 Pt 3:9). As Jacob inherited from Isaac the divine blessing, and Isaac from Abraham, so we inherit through Christ the blessing of the Father. Now, it is as pledge and promise. One day we will hear, 'Come, blessed of my Father, to possess the kingdom' (Mt 25:34).

EPILOGUE

In twelve homilies I have commented on a few sections and various aspects of the Eucharistic Celebration, each in a limited and partial way. I hope such reflections may have helped the reader to a better understanding and a greater appreciation of the Eucharist. But their greatest fruit would be to arouse in readers the desire to continue to study and meditate, using for this purpose works that are more demanding, documented and systematic. For example:

J. A. Jungmann, *The Mass of the Roman Rite: The Origins and Development*, New York 1951-1954; E. J. Kilmartin, *The Eucharist in the Primitive Church*, New Jersey 1965; Idem, *Church, Eucharist and Priesthood*, New York 1981; J. D. Crighton, *Christian Celebration: The Mass*, London 1971; L. Bouyer, *Eucharist. Theology and Spirituality of the Eucharistic Prayer*, Notre Dame 1968; J. Betz, *The Eucharist, Central Mystery*, in *Mysterium Salutis*, IV/2.

INDEX OF SCRIPTURE REFERENCE